The Queer Afterlife of Vaslav Nijinsky

The Queer Afterlife of
Vaslav Nijinsky

KEVIN KOPELSON

STANFORD UNIVERSITY PRESS

STANFORD, CALIFORNIA

1997

Excerpt from "The War of Vaslav Nijinsky" from
In the Western Night: Collected Poems 1965–1990 by Frank Bidart.
© 1990 by Frank Bidart. Reprinted by permission of Farrar, Straus & Giroux, Inc.

Stanford University Press, Stanford, California
© 1997 by the Board of Trustees of the Leland Stanford Junior University
Printed in the United States of America
CIP data appear at the end of the book

FOR MICHAEL BERKSHIRE

✻

ACKNOWLEDGMENTS

I started writing this book on Fire Island with Doug Wingo and finished it in Miami with Mike Berkshire, both dancers I know from the dance. But it may not be one you'll read at the beach, for which I alone am to blame. Once an academic always an academic, as the following friends and colleagues can attest: Diane Middlebrook, who minded my mannerisms; Wayne Koestenbaum, who lent me his red shoes; Anatoly Vishevsky and Natella Voiskounskaya, who checked my Russian facts; Downing Thomas, who checked my French; Chris Reed, who checked my English; Traci Kyle, who checked the rest; Dorothy Austin, who had me write out loud; Philip Brett, Sue-Ellen Case, Susan Foster, and George Haggerty, who had me perform an Unnatural Act; Linda Bolton, Geeta Patel, Tom Simmons, and Max Thomas, who made me glad to work at the University of Iowa; Chris Lane and Marc Stein, who demonstrated the death drive; Ellen F. Smith, who edited the manuscript; and Evan Wolfson, who shouldn't have gone without saying.

K.K.

CONTENTS

All photographs not otherwise credited are copyrighted by the Dance Collection, The New York Public Library for the Performing Arts, Astor, Lenox, and Tilden Foundations.

The Queer Afterlife of Vaslav Nijinsky

Inscription

*I*f Nijinsky were alive today and sane enough to understand my book, he probably wouldn't appreciate it. I say this, not to sustain the strategic self-deprecation of *Beethoven's Kiss*, but because a man who didn't consider himself homosexual might not care to know about his gay reception. Nor would a dancer be very interested in what may turn out to have been, in essence, an intellectual's attempt to approximate vicarious embodiment. Fortunately, and unfortunately, Nijinsky isn't alive. I'd kill to watch him dance, of course, but am relieved to be unable to write for him. Instead, I inscribe *The Queer Afterlife of Vaslav Nijinsky* to you who, like me, are haunted by a figure you've never seen in motion and wish to know why.

Although I can't write for—or to—Nijinsky, I can, to cite Roland Barthes, "write" him. Nijinsky is an open text. Many of his gestures invite multiple readings, the final gestures in particular. Like Madame de Rochefide, and like *Sarrasine* itself, the Balzac novelette that gives her the final word, Nijinsky, even in closing, remains pensive—readable according to the codes of classical ballet and modern dance, yet not contained by them. It may be that Nijinsky alone, who devised an idiosyncratic system of dance notation few can decipher, knew—or thought he knew—what these gestures meant. But since we can't read his mind and wouldn't limit ourselves to his self-interpretation if we could, it's up to us to trace his gestural trajectory. It's up to us to transcribe and, if necessary, reconstruct

3

our impressions of Nijinsky—plastic as well as psychic, ascetic as well as aesthetic, because he shaped the way we've both envisioned and enacted, in both fine art and daily life, gay or, to be postmodern, queer identity.

Why trace the gestural trajectory, as opposed to describing spatial patterns or picturesque attitudes? Most of us read dance as mimetic—even dance not meant to be. The dance in question was meant to be. Working in the wake of choreographers who conceived of classical ballet in terms of expressive movement (Jean Georges Noverre, the innovator of *ballet d'action*, and Michel Fokine, its renovator), Nijinsky captivated audiences who, with his help, learned to conceive of modern dance in similar terms. No wonder our significant impressions, including ones not based on direct observation of Nijinsky dancing, concern unconventional gestures we know, think, or imagine he made. True, many of Nijinsky's patterns and attitudes were equally unconventional. It's just that we don't read them as well and can't see how they signify in a particularly gay way.

But why, given that most of his followers weren't gay, describe Nijinsky's queer afterlife? Nijinsky was the Lord Alfred Douglas of the Ballets Russes. The dancer, however, had even more lilac-hued notoriety than the dilettante who, having lauded the love that dare not speak its name, landed Oscar Wilde in Reading Gaol—notoriety based upon common knowledge of his relationship with Serge Diaghilev, upon his having been one of the first sensuous young men to dominate a Western stage recently riven by the homosexual/heterosexual division we're still contending with, and upon his mastery of leading roles and body languages that had little to do with conventional masculinity. Notoriety, moreover, that few of the gay dancers who've worked in Nijinsky's wake, including Rudolf Nureyev and Michael Jackson, have matched.

And what does it mean to say that Nijinsky, like Wilde, haunts gay identity or that he's had a queer afterlife? It doesn't mean he originated us, in the way that simple-minded psychoanalysts trace adult male homosexuality to aberrant oedipal scenes or lesbianism to isolated instances of childhood sexual abuse. It does mean that his gestural trajectory is a series of events in relation to which one should cultivate a complicated sense of nostalgia, but that one should hesitate to decontextualize. If I seem to decontextualize them here, it may be that one of us, against his better judgment, is still too invested in creation myths. However, it may be that I alone can't think of a more (or less) original way to resist the erasure of all such gay events, whether at the instance of postmodern friends who have sufficient reason, if insufficient desire, to learn something about pre-queer history or at the instance of homophobic enemies who, to throw shade where shade is due, can't have read this far, if at all.

St. Petersburg, *1905*

MUSIC: KADLETZ

LIBRETTO: IVANOV

CHOREOGRAPHY: FOKINE

Acis et Galatée

*W*hat was it like to have been one of the noblemen, perhaps Prince Pavel Lvov himself, who, accustomed to cruising conventionally beautiful boys enrolled in the Imperial Ballet School, suddenly saw an unconventionally beautiful seventeen-year-old faun somersault across the stage at the end of an academic demonstration of classical choreography? Did he say to himself, "This kid is acting like an animal?"—one reading Fokine intended. Or "He's acting like a kid?"—the other intended reading. Which behavior, in general, did he prefer? Which, if either, did he prefer sexually? And did that sexual preference determine his reading—one way or the other? (Like panicky men purportedly uninterested in boys, he may have seen male dancers asexually.)

Did young Nijinsky's gesture make our nobleman want to somersault as well? Did it make him think he could? Or should? Did he feel too old to do so? Too out of shape? Too decorous? Too sophisticated? Was the feeling one of regret? One of relief?

Did the gesture make him long for Nijinsky? Or fall for him? Did the gesture make him want to be Nijinsky? And if so, which Nijinsky? Did he suddenly see himself as a ballet dancer who depended upon patronage, including quasi-pederastic patronage? Or did he see himself as a faun? And if so, why? Because he wanted to be carefree? Or as carefree as before? (He could have been killed in the unrest resulting from Bloody Sunday.)

Or did he both love Nijinsky and see himself as Nijinsky? And if so, wasn't that supposed to be narcissistic? Or, in the faun fantasy, did he see himself as both man and beast? Both man and god? And if so, wasn't that supposed to be homosapient? Or to be homosexual? Was there any difference? Had there been one in ancient Greece? Or ancient Rome? And what was a Roman faun doing in a Greek ballet?

Somersaults, per se, signified metonymically: tumbling, gymnastics, acrobatics, street shows, carnivals, circuses—lowbrow entertainment, as opposed to imperial ballet. Here, however, they signified metaphorically: joy, bliss, rapture—even in what weren't, for Acis and Galatea, particularly happy circumstances. Ease as well—letting gravity do its thing, as opposed to the vertical thrust of ballet. Difficulty, too—*kuvyrkat'sia*, an expression akin to "jumping through hoops" or "going in circles." But neither sexual ease nor sexual difficulty. Somersaults, in Nijinsky's case, connoted frolic and innocent play. Non-orgasmic—and prepubescent—rapture. (His Parisian faun would never somersault.)

Easy, but somewhat difficult—like skipping, another juvenile skill. Another ludicrous, if pleasant, form of locomotion. (Few adults either skip or somersault.) Easy, but difficult—like prolonged masturbation, another relatively private practice in which getting there is half the fun. Somersaulting is more private than dancing, less private than skipping, and far less private than masturbating—which must have made Nijinsky's maneuver rather upsetting. Why turn a prepubescent and protomasturbatory somersault into a spectacle? And why watch the spectacle? Was our nobleman a voyeur? A Peeping Tom? A

Peeping Tom who wanted to make a spectacle of himself? Or who wanted to be spied upon?

Did he then say to himself, "Will Nijinsky ever look at *me*?" Or at the first curtain call think, "*Look* at me. *Look at me!*"? Prima ballerinas, passive objects of the male gaze, do see us. Danseurs, pandering to the panicky, don't. They gaze at ballerinas. (To cite a critical commonplace, Acis gazes at Galatea, who sees herself being seen.) Did gazing at Nijinsky feminize Nijinsky? Or, insofar as desire is presumptively heterosexual, did it feminize the gazer? Or was he feminized by his futile wish to be gazed upon by Nijinsky? And if both gazer and gazed upon were feminized, or if neither was, what happened to presumptive heterosexuality? What happened to compulsory heterosexuality? Were they destabilized? And if so, to what extent? For how long? Until the final curtain call? Then what?

Did our nobleman remember Nijinsky the next day? And the day after that? And the day after that? Did he obsess? Did he see Nijinsky again? Did he want to meet Nijinsky? Or not want to? And if not, why not?

This book isn't an anatomy of the gay—or, if not gay, homosexual—balletomane. Its focus is both too narrow, excluding dancers other than Nijinsky, and too broad, including Nijinsky lovers who don't love dance. But our nobleman may have been, or may have become, one of the first to fit the pre-Stonewall stereotype. Or not. Maybe the balletomane, like the opera queen, is by definition more interested in female performers than in male performers. Or maybe the stereotypes are incommensurable: one loving only divas, the other only danseurs. And maybe the truly (homosexual) gay man—or the one with truly aristocratic pretensions—is, or used to be, both at once: someone who dreamt of seeing Rudolf Nureyev and hearing Maria Callas. But whatever became of our nobleman, "Whatever became of the likes of him?" is, for the first time in a long time, a question we can and should try to answer.

St. Petersburg, 1906

MUSIC: PUGNI

LIBRETTO: GAUTIER

CHOREOGRAPHY: PETIPA

Le Roi Candaule

*D*iaghilev, to whom Prince Lvov would pass Nijinsky along, never saw him dance *Le Roi Candaule* but did see postcards sold by the Maryinsky Theater of Marius Petipa's Mulatto Slave—if, in fact, the cards record moments within movements Petipa devised. They don't resemble anything Petipa ever had Nijinsky do so much as prefigure things Fokine would have him do as the Golden Slave in *Schéhérazade*. Nijinsky is looking and smiling at a viewer he'd like to grab. His wide eyes indicate intelligence. His parted lips indicate he's about to speak. His tense hands tell us he won't let go. What kind of slave is this? What kind of mulatto slave? And what did Diaghilev make of him?

Anyone looking at a Nijinsky photograph, wrote Edwin Denby, inhabits an imaginary world in which his or her "emotions are not directed at their material objects, but at their imaginary satisfactions" ("Notes" 20). Imaginary satisfactions, however, relate to reality. The reality of the master/slave dialectic, in general, is that masters need slaves to acknowledge them, that slaves know more about masters than masters know about slaves, that slaves resist—and usually resent—masters, and that slaves, too, enjoy (vengeful) imaginary satisfactions. The Russian reality, in particular, is that men like Diaghilev had owned slaves up until 1861, almost none of whom, however, were of African descent. For Diaghilev, the figure of the mulatto, even the Mulatto Slave, was more likely to connote the poetic genius and noble pedigree of Pushkin, a great-grand-son of Peter the Great's favorite blackamoor (Abraham Hannibal), than it was to connote the abject servitude of Uncle Tom. So it would make sense for Nijinsky to look at Diaghilev, acknowledging, quite possibly, his own mastery. It would make sense for Nijinsky to smile at him, marking, quite possibly, fond amusement rather than fierce resentment. It would make sense for Nijinsky to have something to say. And it would even make sense for him to make his move.

But would it make sense for Diaghilev to care to hear what Nijinsky had to say? And, more to the point, would it make sense for Diaghilev to care to have Nijinsky grab him? Like Peter the Great, another extraordinary autocrat, Diaghilev listened to people he considered intelligent but never let underlings push him around. Nijinsky, however, is no ordinary underling. Not only is he made up as a mulatto slave, he's dressed up as a non-Russian slave. In his beaded tunic and feathered headdress, he seems rather exotic and vaguely Eastern—Abyssinian perhaps, like Abraham Hannibal, or possibly Persian, like one of the janissaries in *Schéhérazade*. He seems somewhat barbaric as well, which for an Orientalist like Diaghilev, meant one thing and one thing only: sex. Nijinsky represented the rough, transgressive sex civilized Westerners invented, weren't supposed to want, did want badly, and projected onto alien Others, many of whom they'd colonized. And so Diaghilev would care to have Nijinsky grab him sexually. He'd love, that is, to be "raped"—or at least manhandled—by the Mulatto Slave he'd soon gild.

Or would he? Wouldn't Diaghilev rather rape or manhandle Nijinsky? It's hard to say. We do know Diaghilev had Nijinsky "top" him. We don't know Diaghilev ever topped Nijinsky. But rape fantasies aren't really about rape. And Orientalized man-handlers, ever since the defeat of the Mongol and Ottoman Empires, aren't exactly masculine. Men who imagine being raped are usually into pleasure, not pain, and into power, not powerlessness. Western men who imagine being raped by Orientals are usually the ones doing the emasculating, a tendency that, given Russia's recent defeat in the war with Japan (1904), was complicated by the specific orientation of Nijinsky's facial features—classmates called him the "Little Jap"—but facilitated by his girlish costume and pointy toes. Ballerinas dance *en pointe*; danseurs don't.

And so Diaghilev probably fantasized being in control of a pleasant rape by a feminine, hypersexual, and pseudoservile foreigner he could violate in a painful way should he choose to do so. In other words, he fantasized having been desired by such a person—without having had to seduce him. Diaghilev knows what Nijinsky needs. He needs to screw Diaghilev, or the attractive young man Diaghilev imagined himself to be. (I imagine Diaghilev never looked in a mirror while masturbating—and whether he looked or not may say more about his sexuality than anything else he appeared to do, or cared to do, on the homosexual/heterosexual continuum.) Of course, Diaghilev didn't know anything about Nijinsky at the time and may never have known what Nijinsky needed, which may, in fact, have been to screw Diaghilev in a different figurative sense: the sense in which an ordinary underling would screw his master in return for having been enslaved.

Or at least that's one imaginary satisfaction.

17

Paris, 1909

MUSIC: TCHEREPNIN

LIBRETTO: GAUTIER/BENOIS

CHOREOGRAPHY: FOKINE

SETS AND COSTUMES: BENOIS

Le Pavillon d'Armide

*D*iaghilev, having seen Nijinsky dance *Le Pavillon d'Armide* at the Maryinsky Theater, used the ballet to open his first Paris season. The French, unused to male dancers of Nijinsky's caliber, went wild, deeming him *le Vestris de nos jours*. They were particularly impressed by the unusual height and improbable timing of his *sauts* and *vols*, and by the ease with which he seemed to perform them. Of course, other Russians leapt as well, or nearly as well; so did several Danes. But Nijinsky was the first to leap in such a way onto a Western stage—Copenhagen didn't count—that welcomed the spectacle and sustained the illusion.

Or off of—and all over. Nijinsky may have flown offstage in the pas de trois, an exit that anticipated *Le Spectre de la rose*, and then bounded across the stage in his solo variation, but he first appeared in Paris by walking onstage with two female partners (Tamara Karsavina and Alexandra Baldina). Some found the entrance "curiously modest" (Whitworth 40). Others found it remarkably gay:

Benois took Armida's pearls and gave them to Nijinsky, adding a few diamonds for good measure. We know it is the same necklace because it is worn as high as it will go, right under the chin. (It started a fashion: Cartier copied it.) Nijinsky's very first entry on the stage of the Châtelet, because of his equivocal personality, because of his allure, because he combined the strength of a man with the grace of a woman, because of his frilled and skirted costume, and because of his jeweled choker, had sped this most homosexual of centuries on its vertiginous course. (Buckle 96)

And because of that walk. How do you appear at a party full of strangers? Do you make a fabulous entrance and then hold everyone's attention? Do you grab everyone's attention, but lose it? Do you slink in and hide in a corner? Or like Nijinsky, do you make a modest entrance and then do something shameless: seize control of the verbal field by being witty, charming, or brilliant; control the visual field by looking exotic, glamorous, or beautiful; or upstage the brilliant and beautiful by moving like an athlete, dancer, or fop—or maybe even all three. If Wilde entered Paris flaming, more hard than gemlike and full of false gay pride, Nijinsky entered glowing softly, more pearl than diamond, and secretly fabulous.

No doubt, you probably don't turn Armida's Favorite Slave into a party trick. You probably don't care to take a flying leap in an unfamiliar setting, even if you do know how. Fellow partygoers would think you strange, if not inept. But you might care to leap in the privacy of your own home—or closet. Nijinsky's dancing may not be the sort of thing straight men see themselves doing for a living but it is the sort of thing gay men do when alone or in the company of friends. Harold Acton and Brian Howard, fellow Bright Young Things who hadn't studied ballet, used to listen to gramophone records of Ballets Russes music and "leap into riotous dances" they considered better outlets for their "animal spirits" than the football matches they were forced to play at Eton (Acton 82). Edwin Denby, a dance critic who had studied ballet, used to hold the "poses" in Nijinsky photographs (one of which is a leap!), an exercise involving "unbelievable strain," because they enabled him to oppose "what the body would naturally do" and to imitate his idol's "instinct for countermovement" ("Notes" 17).*

One such countermovement—a curious little twist taken to an extreme in L'Après-midi d'un faune—was cultivated, not instinctive. Nijinsky's épaulement, or placement of the upper body in opposition to the legs and hips, represented a typically Russian refinement, or perversion, of French technique. (Gallic ballerinas faced their audience from head to toe.) But since Nijinsky was the first danseur to appear in Le Pavillon d'Armide, no one except the Russians in attendance knew about épaulement. All they knew, or sensed, was that the Favorite Slave seemed askew. What did that signify to Parisians at the time? Did they read Nijinsky's first step as a limp—a slight disability, pathetic and endearing in one so young? Did they read it as a swagger, sexy and cocky? They read it, or gays did, as a limp. Or so we now imagine. Lincoln Kirstein, looking at the photographs and imagining satisfactions unrelated to Diaghilev's, found that "Nijinsky's pearly apparition, his powerful yet vulnerable presence, moves in an ambience not without its own sadness" (Nijinsky Dancing 71). Of course, Kirstein's reading can't be yoked to épaulement alone. As a balletomane too young to have known them, he was saddened by the loss of

*According to Paul Claudel, Nijinsky didn't exactly hold poses: "He moved like a tiger [and even in repose] seemed imperceptibly to be dancing" (quoted in Reiss 167).

both baroque Versailles (the birthplace of ballet, the setting of *Le Pavillon d'Armide*) and early modern Paris (the birthplace of the Ballets Russes). As a gay balletomane too young to have seen him, he was saddened by the untimely "death," or early retirement, of Nijinsky. Kirstein, however, didn't construe the sad ambience of Nijinsky's vulnerable presence as a function of his own nostalgia and sentimentality. He simply construed it as a function of Nijinsky's *tonnelet*—a costume Kirstein also called "the uniform of a superior order inhabiting a domain outside reality" (*Nijinsky Dancing* 71).*

Kind of like the costumes Michael Jackson wears. Think of his space suit in *Scream* (1995). But the unreal supremacy of the Favorite Slave isn't exactly the unreal supremacy of the Gloved One. Whereas most pop stars are down to earth, all ballet dancers belong to a superior order inhabiting a domain outside reality. They all do impossible things in impossible situations yet look graceful. For Kirstein to have mentioned it, the unreal supremacy of the Favorite Slave must have seemed truly exceptional and truly gay. Kind of like Judy Garland or Mary Martin. Kirstein was old enough to have seen Garland walk into Munchkin Land, an equally famous and equally modest entrance into another, better world claimed by gay men in need of escape—or rescue. He was also old enough to have seen Martin enter Never-Never Land, another, better world claimed by gay men in need of moisturizer. But Martin entered flying. And

*According to Geoffrey Whitworth, the Favorite Slave represented "the supreme functioning of a state of being most strange and utterly alien from our own" (41).

24

so for Kirstein, Nijinsky was Dorothy Gale when he appeared and Peter Pan when he disappeared—carefree, ageless, yet dead.

Of course, who hasn't dreamt of remaining young somewhere over the rainbow? The fantasy is typically—or stereotypically—gay, but essentially human, an expression I, neither humanist nor essentialist, usually avoid. As is the fantasy—or reality—of the secretly fabulous entrance. Or, to be pseudoclinical, the fantasy of the schizophrenic entrance. Like his bipolar Russian roles (man/beast, man/god, master/slave), Nijinsky's Parisian entrance (modest/shameless, walking/flying) suggests the split personality mistakenly associated with the schizophrenia we now know he had. It also suggests, if not Nietzsche's madness—Nietzsche, like Wilde, had syphilis—then the critical division with which the Gay Scientist presented himself to the Western world, a division to which most of us, including most of us who are gay, can relate. Nijinsky entered Paris Apollonian and became Dionysian, a bouleversement Nietzsche would have appreciated. Although he praised Greek tragedy as the Apollonian perfection of Dionysian ritual, Nietzsche saw himself as Dionysus. How do you see yourself? Are you cool, calm, and collected (Apollonian) or wild, crazy, and intoxicated (Dionysian)? Are you Edwin Denby, holding poses you find an unbelievable strain, or Harold Acton, leaping about like a maniac? Are you a bit of both? If so, which one is the real you? Which you predominates? And which do you hold back? Do you present yourself as a sex fiend but then abstain? Do you play hard to get and then let yourself go?

Dance movement, of course, needn't be motivated, and formalists feel it shouldn't be. André Levinson, for example, preferred to see ballet as "extrapsychological" ("O moskovskom balete" 160). But Fokine was no formalist. Having attended the Moscow Art Theater, he replaced hand gesture and facial expression with an expressiveness of the whole body. He also had dancers act like divas, embellishing characters with arabesques of their own personalities. No wonder Levinson disliked *Le Pavillon d'Armide*, which he also faulted for failing to incorporate baroque dance. (The ballet relied on music, sets, and costumes alone to place itself historically and so didn't measure up to *Sleeping Beauty*, a retrospective masterpiece.) Nijinsky, moreover, was Fokine's prize pupil. Like Maria Callas, another diva who found herself in bravura roles, Nijinsky was psychological, a method dancer who cared about characters' motivations and drew upon personal experience to discover them. So if Callas, as Tosca, saw Scarpia as Aristotle Onassis (a claim Franco Zeffirelli has made), Nijinsky, as the Favorite Slave, saw—what? What was he thinking—in character—when he walked onstage? Or more to the point, what did people think he was thinking? As a diva, a queer diva, he may have been thinking about his dazzling leaps. But as the Favorite Slave, he may have been thinking about Diaghilev. "Armida is Diaghilev, the man to whom I belong. What must I do, and how must I do it, in order to sustain his affection? I shall walk like this, indicating that I know my place—and my worth. The women I am with are acquaintances, not friends. Not lovers. They seem to like me, and so I'm polite, courteous, solicitous. That is all. When they leave, I'll amaze him. I'll leap like I've never leapt before—and make *him* know my worth. Or make him remember it. I'm one of these pearls. I'll become, for him, one of the diamonds."

Or did he think, "I am Diaghilev?" Diaghilev, by then, had tried to involve Nijinsky in ménages à trois and may have managed to do so—something people at the premiere suspected.* And so, years before he led his own troupe across the United States, the Favorite Slave may have imagined being his own master. "I am Diaghilev and these are my lovers. I prefer Nijinsky but, because I shouldn't play favorites, try not to show it. They may prefer one another. But I know they need me, and need me to control them, which I try not to show as well. I'm polite, courteous, solicitous—as long as they remember their place." Or again: "I am Diaghilev and love beauty. All beauty—art, music, dance, drama—all at once. These two are beautiful. Look at them, love them, as I do—synesthetically."

Of course, these are two women he is with. But during the entrance, and until the three begin the dance itself, which reflects both the gender dimorphism of classical ballet (men exhibiting strength in large jumps and air turns; women exhibiting quickness, flexibility, and fragility in leg extensions and footwork) and, to a lesser extent, the romantic ideology of ballet narrative (men loving unattainable women; unattainable women redeeming unworthy men), Nijinsky—walking the walk if not talking the talk—is practically one of the girls. Gender ideology, or the embodiment thereof, is suspended. And even after the Favorite Slave begins to dance the pas de trois,

*This became the pretext of *Jeux*, a modern pas de trois in which Nijinsky did play Diaghilev and, because an all-male ensemble would have been outrageous, sandwiched him between two female dancers, one of whom represented Nijinsky.

he still belongs to the unreal world of the unattainable Armida (a tapestry figure who momentarily comes to life) and so, to a certain extent, still belongs to the feminine camp. The soaring solo, which inspired the myth of the birdlike bones in Nijinsky's feet, is another story altogether.

Paris, 1909

MUSIC: TCHAIKOVSKY

CHOREOGRAPHY: PETIPA

SETS AND COSTUMES: BAKST

❧

L'Oiseau d'or

*O*r *is* Nijinsky's soaring solo another story altogether? In homophobic parlance, the unbearable and imaginary lightness of gay being—located in our loafers, in the way we prance—is an indication of abject femininity, if not nongendered disembodiment.* Or so we're told on this side of the Atlantic. When Clifton Webb tested for the role of Waldo Lydecker in *Laura* (1944), the head of casting at MGM told Otto Preminger "He doesn't walk, he flies"—implying, the director needlessly remarks, "that he was effeminate" (73). But when Nijinsky both flew offstage and bounded across the stage in *Le Pavillon d'Armide*, or—especially—when he reappeared later that night in the Bluebird pas de deux from *Sleeping Beauty*, retitled *L'Oiseau d'or*, audience members weren't imagining him levitate. There were, by all accounts, watching him levitate, and levitate with a vengeance. For if the pas de deux reintroduced

---

*See Edelman: "The figuration of gay male effeminacy in terms of 'flying' rather than walking, participates in a distinctive category of types for male homosexuality that includes 'being six feet off the ground,' 'being light in one's loafers,' and 'flitting like a fairy.' In each case homosexuality as a presumed ontology produces its legibility in and on the body: produces it, more exactly, in terms of a *contradiction* in the body's relation to itself. As construed through these various figures, that is, the gay male body seems to enact a certain resistance to its own embodiment, to turn against itself as if refusing the substance, the weightiness, the gravity of bodiliness as such" (206–7).

31

Parisian balletomanes to traditional partnering (the supported adagio), it confronted them for the first time with the formal complexity and technical virtuosity both Enrico Cecchetti, who taught Nijinsky the role, and Petipa required. No one, that is, had ever really seen a man do what Nijinsky did at the end of the pas de deux—breeze through a *diagonale* of *cabrioles* and *brisés volés*, and hence literalize, or seem to literalize, the homophobic figure of gay male flight, which made all the gender difference in the world. For notwithstanding the proclivity of Westerners, even ones on the other side of the Atlantic, to read virtuosic display as feminine (both Edward Said and Jacques Lacan come to mind), Nijinsky's final *diagonale* was read, even by homosexuals who'd internalized the homophobic figure, as the triumphant flight of a manly gay bird.

Now, dance theorists wonder whether the steps in the *diagonale* are, in fact, gestural. Marshall Cohen, for example, calls them "mere twisting and turning in the air" (170). The Rose adagio, he concedes, "may appear to express Aurora's . . . emotion (that is, [it] may be [gestural] in [Susanne] Langer's sense), but what emotions does the Bluebird pas de deux express?" (167). One obvious answer is that Nijinsky, as the Bluebird and for that matter as any aerial character, including the Specter of the Rose, expressed, for us, the emotion—and enabled the vicarious experience—of liberation. Liberation from the force of gravity, of course, but liberation from homophobic constraint as well. ("If happy little bluebirds fly beyond the rainbow, why—oh why—can't I?") Literalizing the figure of gay flight, Nijinsky taught us how to prance with pride—true gay pride—and hence to disfigure, transfigure, and transcend the abjection

32

the figure represents without relying on camp, a more stereo-typically gay transcendence of abjection.

In the course of learning that lesson, however, our elders did face one hurdle. Just where, seeing Nijinsky soar, were they to look? Were they to look at the arms, the most winglike human body part, or were they to look at the legs? Léonide Massine, to whom, in a sense, Nijinsky would pass Diaghilev along, looked at the arms: "To convey the quivering motion of the bird's wings he fluttered his hands at such a dazzling speed that they seemed to have exactly the pulsating action of hummingbirds" (87). (Massine may have been a hand fetishist.) Cyril Beaumont, who saw Nijinsky perform the pas de deux in London, looked at the legs: "He seemed not to touch the ground but to glide forward on air, his feet flashing to and fro in the brilliance of his *brisés* and *cabrioles*" (51). (Beaumont may have fetishized feet.) Carl Van Vechten, the dance critic who discovered Edwin Denby as well as the novelist who recommended the title *Prancing Nigger* (1924) to Ronald Firbank, clearing the hurdle, looked at both arms and legs: "How he danced! Do you who saw him still remember those flickering fingers and toes? 'He winketh with his eyes, he speaketh with his feet, he teacheth with his fingers,' is written in the Book of Proverbs, and the writer might have had [Nijinsky] in mind" ("Russian Ballet" 10). And once again, because you can't be too sacrilegious, hear it said too often, or fetishize too many body parts, what Nijin-sky's hands and feet keep telling us is to *prance*.

Paris, 1909

MUSIC: GLINKA

CHOREOGRAPHY: PETIPA/FOKINE

SETS: KOROVINE

COSTUMES: BAKST/BENOIS/BILIBINE/KOROVINE

⚜

Danse caucasienne

*T*he Russians who recognized Nijinsky's *épaulement* in *Le Pavillon d'Armide* found the finale of the Paris premiere familiar as well. The evening ended with a *lezginka*, a stereotypically gendered tribal dance. Stiff warriors throw their arms from side to side, kick their legs, jump on their toes, and hover over supple maidens who, hiding rapid little steps underneath long skirts, seem to float across the stage. In Slavic parlance the men "soar like eagles" while the women "swim like swans," an idiomatic opposition Russians also apply to ballet but that even the Parisians who found Nijinsky's bones birdlike couldn't have known, couldn't have sustained if they had known (there's little figurative difference between soaring and swimming), and, because Nijinsky, as a Captain, wasn't leaping anymore, wouldn't have approximated. For Parisians, danseurs had to defy gravity to appear airborne.

Nijinsky, on tip-toe but not quite *en pointe*, didn't defy gravity in the lezginka. He neither levitated nor used the gesture, or if not the gesture the step, as the basis of vertical thrust. What then did Parisians, who unlike Russians were unused to seeing danseurs move in that direction, make of Nijinsky's more or less effeminate (faux) pas? And what did they make of it in the context of a finale meant to display male violence and muscularity—if only to justify the display of attractive men in motion or to compensate for the problematic gendering of Armida's Favorite Slave? They read Nijinsky's intermittent toe-dancing as unmarked female impersonation, which is to say they didn't exactly read it. Like unmarked transvestism (think of Rudolph Valentino, Liberace as Valentino, Elvis as Liberace, or Michael Jackson as Elvis), unmarked female impersonation is a titillating transgender performance not designed to be seen as such, not predicated on a costume change, and not intended to enable the performer to pass as a woman. Think of Michael Jackson as Diana Ross or, to invoke unmarked male impersonation, Janet Jackson as Michael Jackson—toeing yet not crossing the gender line. Nijinsky, in the lezginka, may be neither a Swan Maiden, the female role it would take a marked transvestite in Les Ballets Trockadero de Monte Carlo to play, nor a "swan" maiden, the female role against which both Russians and Parisians could tell he'd been opposed, but he is, to use a figure that wouldn't have occurred to Parisians unaware of both the idiom and the impersonation, a maiden-like "eagle"—a virile warrior who, for some reason, keeps doing something or who keeps nearly doing something stereotypically feminine.

Of course, not everyone, not even every gay man, not even every nostalgic gay man, would describe unmarked female impersonation as sexually titillating. Many gay men turn off the camp, or wish their partners would, when trying to be either seductive or seduced. Leo Bersani, for example, complains if "the butch number swaggering into a bar in a leather get-up opens his mouth and sounds like a pansy, takes you home, where the first thing you notice is the complete works of Jane Austen, gets you into bed, and—well, you know the rest" (208). Kirstein associated the sensuality of the lezginka with Nijinsky's provocative "ferocity" (*Nijinsky Dancing* 75) but ignored the most fa-

38

mous feature of the dance—famous because jumping on toes sheathed in soft boots looks painful if not impossible and transgressive if not transgendered. He even denied that the lezginka involves any type of impersonation. The Captain, Kirstein asserted, is "not the imitation of a particular personage but the embodiment of a regional vitality" (*Nijinsky Dancing* 75).

As if regional vitality were ever gender-trouble free. Russians found Moscow masculine but St. Petersburg, their capital, feminine. The French found Russia the way Russians found Persia—feminine—but Paris, their capital, feminine as well. Americans, especially ones who've lived through the Cold War, find Russia both masculine and feminine, militaristic yet artsy, which problematizes Kirstein's complacent suggestion that the Captain is merely as wild as the mountains he's supposed to inhabit. Yet for every Kirstein or Bersani there's at least one gay man who needn't ignore the unmarked female impersonation in the lezginka. Take Bill Watson, fellow Slavophile, Yale Russian Chorus cohort, and traveling companion on the choir's 1979 tour of the Soviet Union. Bill, having been given lezginka boots by a dancer we met in Moscow, ran to our hotel to try them on, claimed they fit perfectly, and, imitating a particular personage (Nijinsky), jumped on his toes—a pose he too chose not to hold. Bill knew ballet and could match *pointe* for *pointe* with any Trockadero transvestive but preferred to approximate Nijinsky's unmarked female impersonation, just as he preferred unmarked female impersonation when seductive. So if Kirstein wasn't haunted by the faux pas in the lezginka, Bill was. As am I, who at this point am more haunted by the friend, now dead, who was haunted by Nijinsky than I am by Nijinsky himself.

Paris, 1909

MUSIC: CHOPIN

CHOREOGRAPHY: FOKINE

SETS AND COSTUMES: BENOIS

❦

Les Sylphides

*L*ike *Sleeping Beauty*, *Les Sylphides* is a retrospective masterpiece. The score, the decor, and the movement style all suggest Paris in the 1830's. Even the newfangled abstraction or plotlessness of *Les Sylphides* is an old-fashioned extraction of the *ballet blanc* or vision scene typical of nineteenth-century ballet structure: narrative, mad scene, vision scene, resolution, divertissement. So when Nijinsky ended the second Mazurka (Opus 67 no. 3) by kneeling, brushing aside a lock of hair with his left hand, and stretching out his right "as towards a vision," one would presume the vision to have been of the past (Buckle 99). Van Vechten, looking to the 1890's as well as the 1830's, presumed so: "As the lover of the sylphs in *Les Sylphides* he is a pale *efféminé*, a Chopiniac, a charming Aubrey Beardsley drawing, a lovely thing in line, and grace, and sentiment" ("Secret" 76). Indeed, it's easy to imagine Nijinsky as Chopin, or as gesturing back toward the emasculated Chopin created by the Victorians, if not quite so easy to imagine him as a Beardsley drawing, because Nijinsky, unlike Isadora Duncan but like male pianists who play the composer, embodied both Chopin and his music.* (Van Vechten may have been thinking of Beardsleyesque drawings of Nijinsky made by George Barbier, some reproduced here.)

*"He is the sport and plaything of the flood of melody," wrote an eyewitness, "dancing not to it, but with it or by it—almost, indeed, *on* it" (Johnson 82). "Nijinsky's transformation of the poeticized Chopin," wrote an imaginary witness, "was a deliberate transformation of aural textures" (Kirstein, *Nijinsky Dancing* 81).

But it's possible to imagine Nijinsky envisioning the future instead. When Kirstein, age nine, missed a Boston appearance, which "denied [him] a glimpse of Nijinsky in the flesh," he happened to see an etching by Troy Kinney, reproduced in *Vanity Fair*, "which for the moment almost filled this gap."

> Nijinsky stood in absolute physical and spiritual balance, profiled in silhouette, clad in the black velvet tunic and full white silk sleeves of the male soloist in Fokine's *Les Sylphides*. There was a deeply mysterious, breathless stasis in his stoic silence, something at once commanding, elegant, and very wild. He was the incarnation of Chopin's sonorities as I heard them from my sister's piano practice, and this etching became an icon to which I constantly referred as the sum of masculine possibility. (*Mosaic* 212–13)

And, Kirstein added, it was that "incandescent echo of Nijinsky's image . . . which determined the flickering vision leading me toward my future" (214).

The oppositions that shape sexualities shaped by Nijinsky, you'll have noticed, are piling up. These sexualities can be either male or female (sum of masculine possibility vs. pale *efféminé*), either Apollonian or Dionysian (vision scenes are restrained, yet Kirstein imagined *Les Sylphides* to be wild), and either retrospective or prospective. More important, because retrospective and prospective idealism are equivalent, they can be either retrospectively realistic or prospectively realistic.* Do

---

*Paradise, whether lost or regained, is paradise—a contention Proust contests: "The true paradises are the paradises that we have lost" (*Time Regained* 903).

you dwell upon the past as it probably was? (For gays, this can be traumatic.) Do you dwell upon the future that might, in fact, be? (For gays, this can be traumatic.) Or do you do neither? Like Walter Pater, you may focus on the here and now, living moment by moment. Denby did so, or seems to have done so when looking at Nijinsky photographs, including ones of *Les Sylphides*; photos, he writes, in which Nijinsky's plastic sense never suggests anything as romantic as "a private yearning into an infinity of space"—one way or another—and in which Nijinsky himself, poised between past and future, "seems to be thinking, I've just done that, and then I do that, and then comes that; so the body looks like a face lighting up at a single name [Chopin, perhaps] that evokes a whole crowd of remembered friends" ("Notes" 20; "Carmen Amaya" 90).

A less sympathetic critic would suggest that Denby's synthetic reading—a synthesis of past and future—is a function of *Les Sylphides*'s unfortunate aesthetic. Tim Scholl, who doesn't consider *Les Sylphides* a retrospective masterpiece, calls the work a "peculiar combination of innovation and false nostalgia—furthering the ballet's abstract expressive possibilities while scaling back its technique" (64).* But *Les Sylphides* is synthetic, or synesthetic, in another sense as well. Like every ballet produced by Diaghilev, it aims at being a total art work (*Gesamtkunstwerk*), combining music, dance, and visual art. To perceive Nijinsky reaching out as toward a vision, then, is to hear Chopin's final cadence, to see Fokine's final gesture, and

*Claudel anticipated Scholl. "The only thing worse than bad taste," he wrote with respect to *Les Sylphides*, "is perfection in the midst of bad taste" (quoted in Buckle 389).

to enjoy Alexandre Benois's design all at once—an experience which, in the best of circumstances, can be overwhelming and hard to sustain.* In other words, the synesthetic experience of the total art work can be orgasmic and blissful. But it can be isolated, isolating, and hence somewhat sad as well. The gay man who so experiences Nijinsky—a soloist who, as will be seen, didn't partner very well—is, like the gay man who dwells upon a traumatic past or like Aschenbach in *Death in Venice*, "a solitary [who] has mental experiences which are at once more intense and less articulate than those of a gregarious man [and] never without a melancholy tinge" (Mann 25). So it's a good thing the experience is hard to sustain. It's selfish, it's depressing, and, to be blunt, it's insufferable. For if you've ever known anyone who actually enacts the program Pater recommends, living in a continual present of intense aesthetic experience, you'd realize you don't want to be around, let alone to be, the kind of person who devotes all his time to, say, Nijinsky—if only because his conversation is, if not exactly inarticulate, limited.

*These particular circumstances were less than ideal. Even Benois, according to Kirstein, "felt that Nijinsky's long blond wig and white sheer tights over such massive thighs were faintly ridiculous" (*Nijinsky Dancing* 81).

46

Paris, 1909

MUSIC: ARENSKY/GLINKA

LIBRETTO: PUSHKIN

CHOREOGRAPHY: FOKINE

SETS AND COSTUMES: BAKST

Cléopâtre

*S*ome gay men are snobs. We cultivate aesthetic sensibilities—whether highbrow or lowbrow—we think we need to join social clubs that never really admit us and then lord those sensibilities over others, including other gays. The opera queen devoted to Maria Callas is one such snob. The show queen devoted to Barbra Streisand is another. But artistic tastes, irrespective of the pretensions they enable, are invaluable. They occasion experiences—whether psychic or somatic—worth having and that do, in fact, require investments in cultural capital.

Homosexuals who saw Nijinsky play the Favorite Slave in *Cléopâtre* had such an experience, but they also found themselves playing pretentious roles a heterosexual yet equally snobby observer thought they couldn't carry off. The observer is Ezra Pound, a modernist who wasn't especially homophobic. The observation is versified in "Les Millwin" (1913):

The little Millwins attend the Russian Ballet.
The mauve and greenish souls of the little Millwins
Were seen lying along the upper seats
Like so many unused boas.

The turbulent and undisciplined host of art students—
The rigorous deputation from "Slade"—
Was before them.

With arms exalted, with fore-arms
Crossed in great futuristic X's, the art students
Exulted, they had beheld the splendours of *Cleopatra*.

And the little Millwins beheld these things;
With their large and anaemic eyes they looked out upon
    this configuration.

Let us therefore mention the fact,
For it seems to us worthy of record.

The Millwins, notwithstanding literary criticism that reads them as "a bourgeois family enjoy[ing] art for . . . the wrong ends" (Tytell 133–34), are gay men (hence their mauve and greenish, or Wildean, souls) sitting in poor seats and reacting, trying to react, or thinking they should react the way the art students are. Not that Pound sees the students as more informed or less anemic than the Millwins. Russian ballet—effeminate and popular—wasn't what Pound considered culture. And so, as usual, the modernist would have himself alone both appreciate art and create it.

But you can do other things with art, things Pound rarely attempted. To quote Wilde, you can "either be a work of art, or wear a work of art" ("Phrases" 1206). Pound implies that gay men choose—or can't but choose—to do both. Our Wildean souls were lying along the upper seats like unused boas because Nijinsky used a boa—or veil—in his pièce de résistance: a pas de deux with Karsavina.* For Pound and perhaps ourselves, we

---

*The duet signifies the sex Cleopatra (Ida Rubinstein) and Amoun (Fokine), her victim, are having offstage. See Buckle: "Cleopatra draws [Amoun] towards her couch. They are showered with flowers and their embraces are now hidden, now revealed by the waving draperies of Cleopatra's maidens. It is left to others to express in dance the ecstasies which are being enjoyed on the couch. First, to the Turkish dance from Glinka's 'Russlan,'

were being, or becoming, as well as wearing Cleopatra's Favorite Slave—or, in a metonymic substitution, his veil. *Cléopâtre*'s boa, then, wasn't unused. We used it to convince ourselves that we could move like Nijinsky—or that, like Rubinstein, we could make love to Fokine. Even Pound may have used it, imagistically and unconsciously, to convince himself that he too could do so. And as for the role of art student, perhaps the Millwins couldn't carry it off. (Pound isn't necessarily wrong.) Perhaps they could. (Some of the Slade deputation must have been gay.) What matters is whether they felt they could and what they performed in that capacity, two subjects on which the poem is silent. Did the Millwins, like the students, cross their arms inadvertently because they too exulted? Or did they do so deliberately, to impress upon people like Pound that although their seats were poor, their tastes weren't?

Karsavina and Nijinsky perform a bounding number with a golden veil. As he lifts her from side to side the veil describes a loop or arch in the air" (103).

Berlin, 1910

MUSIC: SCHUMANN

LIBRETTO: FOKINE/BAKST

CHOREOGRAPHY: FOKINE

SETS AND COSTUMES: BAKST

❧

Carnaval

Nijinsky took over as Harlequin not because he wasn't very good as Florestan, the character who represents Schumann's gregarious, headstrong, and impulsive side, but because he was even better at being a little bad.* Nijinsky's "unforgettable" Harlequin, to quote Geoffrey Whitworth, was "a sly fellow, slickly insinuating, naughtily intimate [and] saved from viciousness only by his unerring sense of fun." He was, in fact, "the very soul of mischief—half Puck—but Puck with a sting, and with a body like a wire of tempered steel" (46–47). Cyril Beaumont, equally enchanted, considered him to be as "lively as Mercury and as maliciously mischievous as Tyl" (24).† Van Vechten thought that Nijinsky's "memorable" Harlequin suggested "roguishness and impertinence" ("Secret" 77). Kirstein thought the photographs suggest "prankishness, slyness, waggish irony, with a tinge of malice" (*Nijinsky Dancing* 95).

None of these descriptions amounts to a gay stereotype. Nor are they stereotypical in any other sense of the word. For if Nijinsky, unlike his cohorts in *Carnaval* who represent familiar types from the commedia dell'arte, isn't "at all the blustering, magnificent Harlequin of Italian comedy" (Whitworth 46), nei-

*Schumann was a manic depressive who thought he had a split personality. "Eusebius" represented his solitary, dreamy, and romantic side.

†Jean Cocteau, disenchanted because Nijinsky wouldn't give him the time of day, called him "a sort of middle-class Mercury, an acrobat cat stuffed full of candid lechery" (quoted in Kirstein, *Nijinsky Dancing* 95).

ther does he reduce to any other stock figure (Puck, Mercury, Tyl)—which may have been what Whitworth and company found unforgettable. Barthes would have found it so. He devoted his professional life to escaping the prisonhouse of stereotypes, probably because he found gay stereotypes, especially ones that feminize men, inaccurate. Had Barthes seen Nijinsky's Harlequin, then, he too would have applauded—and remembered—the way the dancer expressed the perverse truth of his unconventional character. This would apply to Nijinsky's Tyl as well.

But how did Nijinsky manage to express that truth? How did he convey it in motion? Like a novelist who creates realistic characters by giving them more and more irreconcilable attributes, Nijinsky gave Harlequin more and more irreconcilable movements. This is especially true of the "Paganini" solo, where Nijinsky realized Fokine's romantic interpretation in a dazzling and self-contradictory display of head wagging, finger pointing, hand clapping, and *batterie* (*cabrioles*, *entrechats*, *pirouettes*). Nijinsky's revision of Petipa's "Bluebird"—double-timing the hand fluttering—is an analogous realization. For it was the increased frequency of activities that, even in combination, had very little to do with one another—clapping hands and twinkling toes say very different things about a performer—which made Harlequin's *diablerie*, according to Kirstein, "gayer, crueler, and more provocative" (*Nijinsky Dancing* 95). No wonder Kirstein claimed to find waggish irony—double-meaningfulness almost impossible to convey without words—amidst the flurry of Nijinsky's characterization.

Why, then, do Nijinsky's spectators and imaginary spectators—assuming they have a Barthesian interest in their subject, an all too true hence somewhat false assumption in my case—focus on his final gesture as well, on the moment when the flurry subsided? Beaumont, for example, exclaimed that when Nijinsky ended the solo by executing a *grand pirouette à la seconde*, spinning more and more slowly, and sinking "unflurried" into a cross-legged sitting position, "his dancing was music made visible" (24), an echo of a review published in *The Times*: "Nijinsky dances with incredible virtuosity during the number 'Paganini,' and at the wonderful point where the dominant seventh on E flat emerges by the deft use of the pedal, the dancer represents the effect to absolute perfection by suddenly sitting down" (June 22, 1911).* Is it, in the final analysis, that they're glad to see him settle down even if, like any discourse, he has no choice but to settle into stereotype? (But into which stereotype does Nijinsky's Harlequin settle? Puck? Mercury? Tyl?) Or is it that they're glad to be startled anew, just when they'd expected typical closure? After all, no classical danseur would end a solo by sitting down, just as no classical composer would end on anything but the tonic. And so Nijinsky's Harlequin never really becomes stereotypical. Like both Petrouchka (a startling combination of Punch and Pierrot) and Tyl (a startling combination of Harlequin and Robin Hood), he remains thoroughly unsettled—and unsettling.

*Hugo von Hofmannsthal claimed that "Schumann's music is [the key to the ballet]. Each moment of *Carnaval* seems to well up spontaneously from its score" (3: 146). Charles Rosen asserts that "the musical idea [in 'Paganini'] *is* the pedal effect" (25).

Paris, 1910

MUSIC: RIMSKY-KORSAKOV

LIBRETTO: FOKINE/BAKST/BENOIS

CHOREOGRAPHY: FOKINE

SETS AND COSTUMES: BAKST

Schéhérazade

*T*he Golden Slave in *Schéhérazade* was Nijinsky's fourth such role. He'd been the Mulatto Slave in *Le Roi Candaule* and the Favorite Slave in both *Le Pavillon d'Armide* and *Cléopâtre*. People noticed the pattern. "How odd it is that Nijinsky should always be the *slave* in your ballets," Walter Nouvel told Diaghilev, "I hope one day you'll emancipate him" (quoted in Buckle 124). They also noticed that it was the first time Nijinsky died on stage. Or rather, the first time he'd been killed— slain, along with all but one of the other revelers, by the Sultan's janissaries. (The Sultana, danced by Ida Rubinstein, a notorious Salomé, kills herself.) The death of the Golden Slave, however, is no mere death. It's a tragic early gay death and thus like Salomé's *Liebestod*—in the play by Wilde, if not the opera Strauss based upon the play—has distinctly heteroerotic, homoerotic, and homophobic overtones. To cite an erotic-minded and death-driven enthusiast, "[Nijinsky] put such beauty into [his death] that we became amorous of death" (Ricketts 175). To cite a phobic-minded and life-affirming critic, "he has to be punished . . . for being the erotic subject of the (male) spectator's gaze" (Burt 85).

But how does the death of the Golden Slave in *Schéhérazade*, another total art work, signify synesthetically? To what extent are these overtones musical (aural)? To what extext are they decorative (visual)? To what extent are they narrative (diegetic)? And to what extent are they gestural (kinetic)?

For Kirstein, an erotic-minded and synesthetic critic, the

love portion of Nijinsky's *Liebestod* was fundamentally musical: "In *Schéhérazade*, Nijinsky moved in three dimensions, muscle against lurid color on top of heavy-breathing orchestration" (*Nijinsky Dancing* 99). For Denby, a like-minded critic, "the 'Slavic harmonies' of Rimsky's score dunked the orgy on stage in a bath of gold" ("Schéhérazade" 240). For Acton, a phobic-minded enthusiast, the death portion was also fundamentally musical: "To me, [*Schéhérazade*] was one of the most memorable of Diaghileff's ballets: the heavy calm before the storm in the harem: the thunder and lightning of negroes in rose and amber; the fierce orgy of clamorous caresses; the final panic and bloody retribution: death in long-drawn spasms to piercing violins" (113). The two orgy references are accurate. Diaghilev had renamed and reprogrammed "Festival at Baghdad: The Sea," the final section of Rimsky-Korsakov's symphonic suite, "Orgy: Slaughter." Acton's reference to piercing violins, however, is somewhat misplaced insofar as it is Rubinstein, not Nijinsky, who dies with strings attached. The Golden Slave dies just after brass blare; the Sultana dies while the concertmaster plays her leitmotif one last time. The misplacement is nonetheless understandable. Not only, as will be seen, do the Sultana and her Golden Slave share certain characteristics, the tune the brass blare is a reduction of that leitmotif as well. What we hear, then, as the slave dies is the musical essence of his mistress.

Denby, "dazzled . . . by the sensual shock of [Leon Bakst's] brilliant décor" ("Schéhérazade" 240), understood Nijinsky's *Liebestod* in visual terms too, a function of the Fauvist color scheme Kirstein called lurid, associating it with his development of "preferences beyond . . . 'good taste'" (*Mosaic* 212), and of the Orientalism Westerners find sexy.* To quote Levinson, who, insofar as *Schéhérazade* is more symbolist than naturalist and hence more or less extrapsychological, did appreciate the ballet: "This ardent and cruel magnificence of color, this effluvium of sensuality which emanates from the setting produces an action in which the very excess of passionate ecstasy can only be satiated by the spilling of blood" (*Bakst* 158). But unlike the Mulatto Slave, the Golden Slave—for Parisians, if not Russians—was both primitive and Oriental. In other words, if the Mulatto Slave seemed rather civilized to Diaghilev, reminding him of Pushkin, the Golden Slave seemed rather barbaric to Proust, or to Proust's compatriots, reminding them of full-blooded Africans.† To quote Glenn Watkins: "Noting the effect of the mise en scène upon those who were given to making hollow distinctions among the Russian ballets, Proust provided testimony of the natural tendency to fusion between Orientalism and Primitivism by observing that some were tempted to claim

---

*Bakst combined blue, green, and orange and used Turkish, Persian, and Mogul design elements.

†The Golden Slave wore dark blue body paint "not unlike the bloom on black grapes" (Beaumont 35). According to Fokine, however, the Golden Slave was "a primitive savage, not by the color of his body make-up, but by his movements. Now he was a half-human, half-feline animal, softly leaping great distances, now a stallion, with distended nostrils, full of energy, overflowing with an abundance of power, his feet impatiently pawing the ground" (156). Following Fokine's gendered imagery, Benois called the Golden Slave "half-cat, half-snake, fiendishly agile, feminine and yet wholly terrifying" (quoted in Buckle 141).

Schéhérazade as a kind of *art nègre"* (67).* But if Proust himself never displayed that tendency to fusion, like Levinson he did appreciate the symbolic dimension of *Schéhérazade*'s Orientalism. Or rather, he appreciated its semisymbolic dimension. For if the ass Charlus thrusts outward (in *Cities of the Plain* 890) seems "almost symbolic" to gays in the know, the one the Golden Slave thrusts upward, a description I'll soon clarify, seems so as well—although, unless every rectum is a grave, as Bersani would have it, in a different sense of the symbolic.†

Most of us, however, find the narrative ended by "Orgy: Slaughter" remarkable. After all, tragic early death is always already literary, even when orchestrated or visualized. Tchaikovsky's "Romeo and Juliet" Overture, for example, is based on Shakespeare and Michelangelo's *Pieta* on Scripture. In *Schéhérazade*, the Golden Slave is the last to be released from captivity (he springs to life from behind a third blue door), the only one to captivate the Sultana, the only one nearly to escape the janissaries, and the last one to be killed by them. The symbolism of this naturalist narrative, however, calls into question whether the Golden Slave is really captivated—by being either kept by the Sultana or

---

*See Proust: "Even those society people who professed to be endowed with taste and drew otiose distinctions between the various Russian ballets . . . were almost prepared to attribute [*Schéhérazade*] to the inspiration of Negro art" (*Captive* 238).

†Proust saw Charlus, a homosexual love-slave, as Diaghilev and Morel, a bisexual violinist, as Nijinsky: "A manager modest in regard to his true merits, [Charlus] contrived to place [Morel's] virtuosity at the service of a versatile artistic sense which increased it tenfold. Imagine a purely skilful performer in the Russian Ballet, trained, taught, developed in all directions by M. Diaghilev" (*Cities* 941–42).

killed by the Sultan. In other words, for anyone attuned to the symbolism, Nijinsky is a free agent, whatever his psychological motivation or final fate may be. Metaphysically speaking, he is the beleaguered individual who can't be taken, the blithe spirit who embodies the license, including the sexual license, Westerners fantasize. Or to quote Lynn Garafola, making the fusion Proust and Watkins deplore, "a primitive who from the moment he bolted onstage until the final spasm of his death exalted the fully liberated self and its inevitable clash with society"—a "fully actualized being" who, notwithstanding the naturalism Fokine tried to attain, both "disavowed psychology" and "demarcated a psychic space where id transgressed and triumphed" (*Diaghilev* 32, 34). So is the Specter of the Rose, according to Garafola.

Needless to say, the meaning of Nijinsky's first performative death is generated by other such oppositional and primarily narrative differences. For example, in addition to signifying in between symbolic enfranchisement and naturalist disenfranchisement, a signification with little gay connotation, the Golden Slave also signifies, gayly, in between his spectacular entrance and equally spectacular exit. The entrance is a curiously immodest opening of a closet door—one Beaumont describes as "the kind of leap a tiger might make" (35)—whereas the exit is a curiously immodest refusal to reenter the closet.*

---

*Most characters, even drama queens, go out the way they come in. The Specter of the Rose, for one, leaps out the open window he leapt in, a more structurally satisfying because perfectly symmetrical denial of the closet thematic the Golden Slave invokes in order to enact fatal gay liberation. Of course, no orgiast slain in *Schéhérazade* goes out the way he or she comes in. Nor does the Sultana.

The Golden Slave also signifies in between savagery and civility, a semiotic situation anticipated by the Mulatto Slave and typical of Russia in general, for non-Russian Orientalists, and of the Ballets Russes in particular. As Peter Wollen points out, the Diaghilev ensemble was "both 'ultra-natural' (wild, untamed, passionate, chaotic, animal) and 'ultra-artificial' (fantastic, androgynous, bejewelled, decorative, decadent)" (27). Which is to say that one of the things that makes Nijinsky, as the Golden Slave, gay makes him both balletic and Russian as well. All three orientations negotiate the ultra-natural/ultra-artificial contradiction.

Another such contradiction is the oppositional difference of gender—the androgynous collapse of which difference Wollen mistakenly calls artificial.* Once again, the Golden Slave signifies in between masculinity and femininity—a semiotic situation located in between *Schéhérazade* and other ballets Nijinsky starred in as well as within *Schéhérazade* itself. All of the roles Nijinsky initiated while sexually involved with Diaghilev occupied both poles at once and hence tended to be read off one another.† As would also prove to be true of the Specter of the Rose and Petrouchka, the Golden Slave cast Nijinsky as an artistic genius—a masculine classification that, paradoxically, authorizes men to express typically feminine emotions. And as would prove to be true of the Faun, the role cast him at

*Both gender difference and the sexual difference presumed to naturalize gender difference are thoroughly—or "ultra"—artificial.

†See Moon: "At the time of *Schéhérazade*, [Nijinsky] was still successfully negotiating the powerful projections of sexual contradiction onto his performances" (62).

the other end of the homosapient spectrum: as an equally paradoxical animal. To quote Michael Moon, a critic given to hosting "Scheherazade parties" of his own: "Both subhuman and superhuman, [the Golden Slave] is simultaneously perceived as an effeminate cat and a tremendous stud, but not as 'masculine' in any ordinary sense" (62). Unless, of course, Beaumont, who describes the entrance as both feline and studly, is more on the mark. Then again, Beaumont is more likely to have denied the femininity of a performance he loved than is Moon, who unlike the Briton never saw Nijinsky live.

The androgyny of the Golden Slave and the meaning of his untimely demise are also located, narratologically, in relation to Nijinsky's previous slaves, their exits in particular.* Notwithstanding the manhandling or rape I fantasize Diaghilev having fantasized in connection with the Mulatto Slave and notwithstanding that he never seems to lay a hand on the Sultana, the Golden Slave is far more aggressive, virile, and hence masculine than his predecessors. Whereas Armida's Favorite Slave, that pearly apparition, acts like a perfect gentleman and whereas Cleopatra's rarely goes near her—the symbolic pas de deux is a far cry from the real sex we imagine Rubinstein and Fokine to be having offstage—the Golden Slave, for all intents and purposes, actually enacts the male rape fantasy the Sultana's male librettists attribute to her.† To quote Acton again,

*The Specter of the Rose, Petrouchka, and the Faun are nonslaves and hence less analogous to the Golden Slave, and because the three postdate him, the Golden Slave couldn't be read through them for some time.

†It's an anticipation of *L'Après-midi d'un faune*. See Garafola: "The partners never touch. They seem to touch, however, and at nearly every point

the Sultana submits to his "clamorous caresses." To quote Van Vechten, "This strange, curious, head-wagging, simian creature, scarce human, wriggled through the play, leaving a long streak of lust and terror in his wake. Never did Nijinsky as the Negro Slave touch the Sultana, but his subtle and sensuous fingers fluttered close to her flesh, clinging once or twice questioningly to a depending tassel" ("Russian Ballet" 9–10).* To quote Kirstein, and note the Diaghilev-like imaginary satisaction, the slavery in *Schéhérazade* is, for the first time, "a lyric metaphor [spelling] ambiguous and provocative servility; ownership licensed willing or unwilling physical possession" (*Nijinsky Dancing* 95). And to quote Garafola: "The Golden Slave ravished rather than courted his mistress; flaunted rather than concealed his body; loosed rather than bridled his physical prowess. Sex incarnate, Fokine's exotic primitive did onstage what respectable men could only do in fantasy" (*Diaghilev* 33). But even though he doesn't seem to touch her and even though he's aggressive, virile, and masculine, the Golden Slave, in yet another symbolic—or imaginary—dimension, does cross over, or pass, into the Sultana's

---

the suggestion of contact is sudden and fraught with violence. Again and again the Faun turns on his prey, locking her in the vise of his powerful arms. Almost always, the throat is the locus of entrapment, as if that exposed column were the gateway to sex itself" ("Nijinsky" 9).

*The Golden Slave did, in fact, touch the Sultana in their supported adagio. Van Vechten's misimpression, however, appears to have been common. According to Francis de Miomandre, for example: "Without ever touching, his feverish hands run over her from brow to ankle with so exquisite a shudder and so deep a sense of the loveliness of desire that we are almost haunted" (5).

feminine camp. Or rather, into her femme-fatale and hence androgynous camp. In a bejewelled outfit more outrageous than the Favorite Slave's—the Golden Slave may not wear a skirt, but he does wear harem pants and a brassiere—and hence more of a renunciation of the Great Masculine Renunciation (straight-laced dressing from which men have yet to recover), Nijinsky, like Rubinstein in both *Cléopâtre* and *Schéhérazade*, is Salomean. Both female captor (Rubinstein) and male captive (Nijinsky) represent phallic women, a figure typical of fin-de-siècle literature and visual art. Rubinstein, that is, subjects Nijinsky to her desire and he in turn subjects her to his—which may not be a bad prescription for the happily-ever-after these two can't but should attain.

Within *Schéhérazade* itself, however, Nijinsky and Rubinstein don't exactly occupy the same gender position. When push comes to shove—which, given Fokine's hands-off approach, it never seems to do—Rubinstein is more of a femme fatale than Nijinsky.* This difference is a function of Rubinstein's biological sex, of course, but it's also a function of her unusual height, of the fact that she alone kills herself, suicide being a female malady in 1910, and of her tendency to sit still while Nijinsky runs around. The stasis/kinesis gender opposition is grounded in modern dance history. Whereas Duncan, contrary to popular belief, maintained the static orientation of classical ballet, Ni-

---

*See Wollen: Nijinsky may approximate the "libidinal power of woman, once her desire is released," but Rubinstein, "both petrifying and petrified, castrating and castrated . . . incarnate[s] the phallic woman of the Decadence" (18). Cf. Buckle: "In 'Schéhérazade,' though an embodiment of lust, [Nijinsky] had been in a way more feminine than Ida Rubinstein" (144).

jinsky emphasized its kinetic component.* But the opposition isn't unique to dance history. As everyone in attendance must have known, and this is especially true of *Schéhérazade*'s Anglo-American audience, nice women—and neither the Sultana nor Rubinstein is very nice—weren't supposed to move very much, or signify *jouissance*, during sexual intercourse.

Rubinstein, of course, gets to signify the Sultana's naughty *jouissance* otherwise. Her stasis, in fact, symbolizes antihomophobic resistance far more effectively than it symbolizes sexual repression. Nijinsky, leaping about like a maniac, simply isn't "permitted to signal anything like Rubinstein's 'majestic' and overwhelming gesture of prolonged motionless resistance to the murderous violence that furiously manifests itself in the piece's last scene" (Moon 64).† Yes, antihomophobic—even in the context of a heteroerotic orgy. Moon is more concerned with gay rehearsals of the final orgy—and with one performed by a friend named Mark in particular—than with the ballet itself: "I take the 'Scheherazade party'—the conspicuous energies with which it is enacted as well as the phobic violence with which it is repressed, violence of either the explosive variety that Mark experienced or the corrosive kind that gradually disabled Nijinsky—as an emblematic expression of a perilously highly charged

*Even in repose, to quote Claudel again, Nijinsky "seemed imperceptibly to be dancing." Nijinsky, however, would come to embrace Duncan's aesthetic, which she claimed to have based on ancient Greek art, in *L'Après-midi d'un faune*.

†Moon is referring to Fokine's description of the Sultana's penultimate gesture: "She majestically awaits her fate—in a pose without motion" (quoted in Wollen 20).

compromise, the energies of which both 'sides' in the ongoing war for and against gay visibility, homophobic and homophile, have been effectively exploiting for most of this century" (65). But setting aside Moon's problematic conflations—of Nijinsky and the Golden Slave, both disabled by homophobia, and hence of homophobia and schizophrenia—and bracketing his important focus on gay rehearsals of *Schéhérazade*, it is nonetheless true that the eroticism of *Schéhérazade* itself is both homoerotic and heteroerotic, and the violence of the finale both homophobic and heterophobic. In this regard, the ballet has as much in common with *Salomé* as it has with *Cléopâtre*, a more obvious pretext. The Sultana's homoerotic feelings for the Golden Slave correspond with Salomé's homoerotic feelings for Jokanaan as well as with Cleopatra's heteroerotic feelings for Amoun. The Sultan's homophobic murder of the Golden Slave corresponds with Herod's homophobic murder of Salomé as well as with Cleopatra's heterophobic murder of Amoun.

Given these internal differences—Rubinstein's majestic immobility as opposed to Nijinsky's manic flight in particular—it may surprise you that many gays, including Moon, think both the Golden Slave and the Sultana resist the Sultan's homophobic violence—indeed, think the Golden Slave alone, symbolically speaking, liberates himself from it even though he's the one who's killed and she's the one who takes her own life. What enables this counterintuitive and wish-fulfilling reading is Nijinsky's final gesture and the kinetic, or hyperkinetic, overtones it manages to produce. The gesture is tripartite. The Golden Slave, in closing, makes a spectacular leap (defying gravity), turns a series of somersaults (letting gravity do its thing), and then does something hard to describe and even harder to imagine. He ends his final somersault by spinning on and leaping off of the back of his neck. Think of break dancing. The thrust, as noted in passing, is upward—gravity-defying. The maneuver is dangerous—death-defying. Think acrobatics.*

And the beauty of this gravity-defying, death-defying, and thoroughly unballetic *Liebestod* is transcendent. Think *Tristan und Isolde*. To quote Van Vechten, "Pierced by the javelins of the Sultan's men, the Slave's death struggle might have been revolting and gruesome. Instead Nijinsky carried the eye rapidly upward with his tapering feet as they balanced for the briefest part of a second straight high in the air, only to fall inert with so brilliantly swift a movement that the aesthetic effect grappled successfully with the feeling of disgust which might have been aroused" ("Russian Ballet" 10). Or more to the point, to quote Francis de Miomandre: "The transport of his movements, the encircling giddiness, the dominance of his passion reached

---

*At a Buenos Aires performance, people thought Nijinsky had really hurt himself and "rose with a scream," according to Nijinsky's wife Romola, when "in that final jump, Vaslav, with the briefest touch of his head on the floor, flung himself into the air by the action of his neck-muscles, quivered, and fell" (313). Londoners were less alarmist. See Beaumont: "It was a thrilling experience to see him now darting this way and that, now doubling on his pursuers in a desperate, frenzied anxiety to escape the avenging scimitars. But a blade flashed and he fell headlong, to spin on the back of his neck with his legs thrust rigid in the air. Then the body fell, rolled over, and was still. This simulated death scene invariably aroused a storm of well merited applause, for, apart from the rare skill obviously essential to its performance, it looked dangerous in the extreme" (36).

such heights that when the executioner's sword pierced him in the final tumult we no longer really knew whether he had succumbed to the avenging steel or to the unbearable violence of his joy in those three fierce somersaults" (3–4). To which there is little one can add, except that the phrase "the unbearable violence of his joy" may be the pithiest conflation of homophobia and homoeroticism ever uttered.

When I call the gesture gravity-defying, I don't mean weightless. Unlike the flight of Nijinsky's Bluebird and unlike, as will be seen, the flight of the Specter of the Rose, the weightlessness of the Golden Slave, is challenged—indeed, tempered—by the downward thrust of the somersaults and by the steel of the scimitars. Oddly enough, it is *Schéhérazade*'s first straight reenactment—as opposed to its gay rehearsals, including Mark's—that tricks us into conceiving the Golden Slave, or at least into conceiving one of his reincarnations, to be weightless. In other words, that has us reimagine gay male flight, if not gay male prancing, as straight male flight. I'm referring to Douglas Fairbanks Sr., the athletic actor who in *The Thief of Baghdad* (1924) became an athletic dancer. "Watching him move" there, commented Mary Pickford, Fairbanks's wife, "was like watching the greatest of Russian dancers" (quoted in Eyman 301). In *Schéhérazade*, that is. The two texts, the film and the ballet, have similar scenic and costume design—although Fairbanks ditched the bra. And the two male leads have similar body language. As Gaylyn Studlar indicates, it is the Orientalized and feminized body of Nijinsky, with its "grace, gestural nuance, physical submission, and . . . polymorphously suggestive exhibitionism" that Fairbanks emulates in *The Thief of Baghdad* (110). Or

73

rather, it's the bearable lightness of the Golden Slave's gay male being that he emulates—which for some reason didn't seem queer at the time. Fairbanks's gravity-defying motion style— bounding up stairs, bouncing through giant jars, and in the end riding a magic carpet with the woman he loves, a far cry from the conclusion of *Schéhérazade*—enabled his character to scale his way into conventional masculinity and Fairbanks himself to become "the world's most famous filmic exponent of energetic, vital American masculinity" (Studlar 108).

Of course, Fairbanks, in *The Thief of Baghdad*, is no sex slave. He fails to scale the Dionysian heights of *Schéhérazade*— unprecedented heights that account for the ballet's popularity, including its gay popularity. Unprecedented in the world of dance, that is, for who knows what went on in the privacy of late-Victorian homes. Unlike the proper, measured farandole in *Sleeping Beauty*, Fokine's bacchanals, beginning with *Schéhérazade*, "were writhing masses of humanity, orgiastic round-dance responses to symbolist 'communality' in a theater that united performer and audience in dionysian ecstasy" (Scholl 65). In other words, they answered the Nietzschean call for Dionysian theater—with Firbankian if not Fairbanksian consequences for queer individuals who contemplated the communal finale in the privacy of their homes and publicity of their writing. Firbank himself, in *The Flower Beneath the Foot* (1923), put a campy spin on the Sultan's heteroerotic and therefore homosocial jealousy:

"With whom," [Yousef] asked, "sweetheart, were you last dancing?"

"Only the brother of one of the Queen's Maids, dear," Mademoiselle de Nazianzi replied. "After dinner, though," she tittered, "when he gets Arabian-Nighty, it's apt to annoy one a scrap!"

"*Arabian-Nighty*?"

"Oh, never mind!"

"But (pardon me, dear) I do."

"Don't be tiresome, Yousef! The night is too fine," she murmured, glancing absently away towards the hardly moving trees. (14)

Denby, in a review of an inferior revival, "wonders what *Schéhérazade* could have looked like when it scandalized our parents or when Parisians swooned at the lushness of [Nijinsky bounding] about . . . like a panther in thrilling spasms that grew to a paroxysm of death at the climax" ("Schéhérazade" 240).[*] I'd like to think Denby had thrilling spasms of his own while pondering the lost production, if not while posing before a bedroom mirror. Kirstein certainly did—while posing as well as pondering. He also had a seminal experience, communal rather than individual, that relates to the unconventional preferences he associates with his exposure in grammar school to *Schéhérazade*'s lurid decor. Kirstein, a young American in Fontainebleau, first learned to liberate his potential, to identify and act on personal goals by "behaving as if something were true even if it wasn't," to push himself to "extreme situations" (quoted

[*]Denby's panther is midway between Benois's feminine cat and Beaumont's masculine tiger.

in Acocella 32), and to embrace the suffering necessary for growth when he witnessed a Fokine-like finale improvised by cult followers of Georgei Gurdjieff, the Armenian spiritualist:

> In one thunderous surge, the entire body of men and women went berserk, and racing, with a startling jump as from a catapult, the whole mass of bodies came hurtling straight at me. I was spared immediate annihilation only when a voice [Gurdjieff's] from the central pavillion yelled "STOP!" The amalgam of bodies froze. . . . The violent collective rush toward me, and the sourceless, shouted "STOP!" gave me a theatrical shudder to which no dance or drama that I had ever seen could compare. It seemed less of a game than a—what? An event? An inexplicable rite? A spectacle? (*Mosaic* 135)

Of course, Kirstein would have compared it with *Schéhérazade*, had he seen the ballet. And, who knows, maybe that—what? event? rite? spectacle?—would have precipitated the self-actualization later prompted by the Fontainebleau farandole. Nijinsky's Golden Slave, after all, did represent a fully actualized being whose role demarcated a psychic space where id transgressed and triumphed. And he too, even when slain, did behave as if something were true—as if he were liberated—even if it wasn't.

The joyous death of the Golden Slave, however, isn't the last thing *Schéhérazade*'s audience, if not its imaginary audience (Denby, Kirstein), sees. They then see the Sultana kill herself. And they then see, as the curtain falls in dead silence, the Sultan weep—weep, moreover, as Herod never does. What were we to think in the end? That the Sultan feels sorry for the Sultana, sorry for having let jealousy get the better of him? That the Sultan feels sorry for the Golden Slave as well, sorry for having let homophobia get the better of him? And did we identify with him? Did we too come to regret homophobia, or not?* Or were we to think the Sultan is sorry for himself alone—the self-pitying tears of the wife beater or gay basher—and hence to think, with more than a little exasperation: "Men! Can't live with them; can't live with them."

Which, oddly enough, is what Michael Jackson enables us not to think. In *Remember the Time*, Jackson's heteroerotic and nostalgic reenactment of *Schéhérazade*, with *Cléopâtre* thrown in to give the video an African cast, the Gloved One, dressed as a golden slave, sings for Pharoah (Eddie Murphy, a notorious homophobe), seduces Pharoah's wife (Iman—now married to David Bowie, a gay icon), is pursued by his henchmen, and, unlike Nijinsky, manages—magically—to escape. At the last possible moment, Jackson spins into a shower of gold, making an uncanny spectacle of himself (we seem to have seen this before, thanks to Diaghilev, Nijinsky, Zeus, and Danaë), of his Midas touch (something Diaghilev could appreciate), of his psychotic if not schizophrenic relation to the Other (could you see him with either Iman or Lisa Marie?), and of his antihomophobic— yes, antihomophobic—foreclosure on the death drive.

If you believe in fairies clap your hands, for only a Peter Pan

---

*The ending of *Salomé* posed a similar problem. Wilde's play enabled people to either approve or disapprove of its homoerotic heroine's execution. See Kopelson 42–44.

could outwit and outlive a Sultan. Only Jackson could do so synesthetically, music videos being today's total art works. And only he could be so pleasing—or blissful—about it. Blissful? Can there be *jouissance,* or *Liebestod,* without an implication of death? Without love? And, in Jackson's case, without sex? I suppose only his boyfriend or plastic surgeon would know for sure—Jackson is both Dorian Gray and Peter Pan, another atypical conflation—because it's possible the performer has a *jouissance* of his own and that his final spin on *Schéhérazade* in *Remember the Time* is a gesture to which gays and queers should attend. It might be the blissful act of a pleasurable and truly liberated body, having nothing to do with the desire we've interrogated to death and having a great deal to do with the future of human sexuality.

Paris, *1910* [*San Jose, 1970*]

MUSIC: STRAVINSKY

LIBRETTO: FOKINE

CHOREOGRAPHY: FOKINE

SETS AND COSTUMES: BAKST/GOLOVINE

❧

L'Oiseau de feu

(FIREBIRD)

*F*okine cast Karsavina and not Nijinsky, despite his aerial ability, as the Firebird. Nijinsky, then, never got to be captured by Ivan-Tsarevich, give him a magic feather, help him kill Kashchei, or bless his marriage to the beautiful Tsarevna. For Wayne Koestenbaum, however, a clothes-conscious poet who grew up in a California suburb, Nijinsky was the Firebird.

Koestenbaum notates what might be called his dance of adolescence in two poems that begin his first collection.[*] In "Shéhérazade"—a reference to Ravel, not Rimsky-Korsakov—Koestenbaum remembers a boyish yet girlish, hesitant yet urgent, and Fairbanksian fantasy of flying yet not flying into sexual maturity.

> A common complaint is that words are not kinetic.
> An Egyptian fag
>   dangles from the rouged lips
> of Reynaldo Hahn—in Proust's bed—
> humming "Si mes vers avaient des ailes."
>   Nothing I can write will have
> such wings. Is there a word in French like "fag"
> for cigarettes, or only in the English of Dick Whittington?

[*]Ned Rorem, as will be seen, calls his first use of Nijinsky "Dance of the Adolescents."

Reynaldo's hair is not more whitened now, there is no
deeper wistfulness
    it can achieve. The art
of sitting still I never learned,
I longed to be the Winged Victory
    seeming to fly but staying
fixed, as slender boys with artistic tastes
molt into husbands, shedding lisps. (5)

            . . .

I, too,

am guilty of magic carpet rides. *Girlish*
    never refers to girls—
only to boys. It's a vast
    waste of breath to call a girl girlish, a boy
boyish. Why does the word "girlish" age
so inconspicuously, show
    so little tarnish, indifferent
to trends in usage, firm to its troubled course? The page

bleakly shimmers as the girlish boy decides,
    at last, to write his tale
of travel, having never
    crossed the border of his own creation,
the fence around his first disaster.
Twenty years ago, in the deep
    of my life, wondering if I could rise
to a bewilderment greater than age eight, I rode

my bike straight into a man who shouted, "Damn girl,
    watch out where you're going!"
He was drunk—so I reasoned—
    to mistake my sex. I enter the boy
I used to be, who lies in my bed,
naked, as if I've purchased him
    from an Arabian sorceress
who sews the body to its sorrow, invisibly. (7–8)

Invisibility is key. In "Fugitive Blue," Koestenbaum describes a series of significant blue accessories (Cub Scouts neckerchief, underwear "stained aqua when the laundry bled" [9], violet shirts luminous enough to "burn the retinas off my class-mates" [10]), including one he'd hoped would help him make a secretly fabulous entrance into his teens.

In seventh grade I bought a kerchief, with a clasp
    To anchor the silk's billowings: I prayed that like an asp

Its azure would sting me into the remoter country
    Where gypsies roamed, their caravans festooned
        along my scarf
Abstractly. I think I imagined the figures, as in palmistry
    One imagines lifelines, or as the larva
Predicts its sapphire wings. I wore this apache
    Scarf the first day of junior high: I thought I was
        Nijinsky,

Purely flame, celestial against the dowdy backdrop
    Of the multi-purpose room. But I'd misread the
        fashion trends:

No one was wearing apache scarves. I ate my meatball slop
    In solitude. The task was not to stand out, but to blend:
Thinking I was invisible, I wore the peacock
    Blue and found I was too visible. I wanted to shock

My public into cheers, until I learned that they were
        primitives,
    Thugs in leather, sluts in midriffs, bike chains
The only organza. Certain blues, like indigo, are fugitive:
    They fade. I never wore the apache scarf again.
Voyages ago I abandoned clothes that now I find,
        ultramarine
    Argosy in which the secret life is fully seen:

I remember now the clothes in which I lost my power.
    The ice blue Nehru shirt that zipped in the back
I wore to the party where I saw Ricky Sowers
    Feel up Carla. But Ricky, too, fought demons: his
        mother smacked
His face on Back-to-School Night. When Carla put her
        hand on Ricky's knee
    I saw my future's blueprint. I was wearing pants of
        lapis lazuli. (10–11)

Koestenbaum—purely flame, celestial—did imagine he was
Nijinsky as the Firebird when he wore that scarf, even though
both psychoanalysis and poetic exigency would have the fan-
tasmatic identification be retroactive and even though a more
obvious tie would have been to Nijinsky as the Faun, another
neckwear fetishist. Nijinsky may rhyme—aslant—with apache,

but Koestenbaum is antipsychoanalytic. "The flaw in primal scenes," according to "Shéhérazade," "is that they / happen, by definition, / only once" (6). And Nijinsky, for anyone refined enough to know about him, as Koestenbaum was, is indeed purely flame, celestial. He is, or was, or should have been the Firebird who'd prevent our loss of power, vanquish the evil in our lives (primitive thugs), and sanctify our marriages to men, should we want them. Luckily, Koestenbaum overcame the sartorial disempowerment commemorated in "Fugitive Blue" and did so, like the Golden Slave, by renouncing the Great Masculine Renunciation. The man, after all, is a visible peacock.

Paris, 1910

MUSIC: ADAM

LIBRETTO: HEINE/GAUTIER/SAINT-GEORGES

CHOREOGRAPHY: CORALLI/PERROT/PETIPA/FOKINE

SETS AND COSTUMES: BENOIS

✼

Giselle

*N*ijinsky, as Albrecht, didn't die in *Giselle* (1841), the romantic ballet par excellence, but he nearly danced himself to death, anticipating the Chosen One in *Le Sacre du printemps* and Moira Shearer in *The Red Shoes* (1948). In other words he approached *Liebestod*, a romantic trope par excellence, without going all the way. (Text of pleasure, Barthes might say, not bliss.) Albrecht, however, is fully romantic insofar as he represents unworthy man redeemed by unattainable woman. Once again, then, Nijinsky fails to connect with a female partner. Physically speaking, he never seemed to touch the Sultana (Rubinstein) in *Schéhérazade*. Metaphysically speaking, he never seems to touch Giselle (Karsavina), the maddened girl who dies of unrequited love for Albrecht, thereby having a unilateral *Liebestod*, and who returns from the grave in a *ballet blanc* to save him from the Wilis.

Physically, of course, Albrecht does touch Giselle, especially in their pas de deux, a number supposed to be "sexually suggestive" and "titillating" (Scholl 47). But according to reliable witnesses, including Karsavina, Nijinsky didn't excel at traditional partnering. His conventional role in *Giselle*, or rather his search for motivation, reduced him to immobility—and not the strategic immobility of the Sultana.* Karsavina writes of one rehearsal:

---

*See Kirstein: "[He] meditated on his own characterization, perhaps trying to discover some psychological relevance to the present time as well as to himself" (*Nijinsky Dancing* 83).

I was sadly taken aback when I found that I danced, mimed, went off my head and died of broken heart without any response from Nijinsky. He stood pensive and bit his nails. "Now you have to come across towards me," I suggested. "I know myself what to do," he said moodily. After ineffectual efforts to go through the dialogue myself, I wept. Nijinsky looked sheepish and unmoved. (220)

An apocryphal report, moreover, has Nijinsky tell her: "I am acting with my eyes!"—behavior George Balanchine would never tolerate. Apparently, Karsavina never forgot this scene nor the poor quality of the performance for which it set the stage. Years later, when coaching Margot Fonteyn in *Giselle*, she realized that Nureyev was "a better dancer than her fabled colleague—less for his purely technical skills . . . than for his variety and his gifts as a partner. . . . 'You are very lucky to have such wonderful partner,' Karsavina told Fonteyn . . . adding, with a sad, downward shake of her head, 'I . . . had Nijinsky'" (Stuart 104–5; final ellipsis in original).*

You'd think Nijinsky's gender-separatist gay fans, especially ones who never saw him dance, wouldn't notice the ineptitude. Why should they mind that straightforward, princely roles weren't his forte? But they did notice and, if I read the denial correctly, they did mind. Where Richard Buckle insists "there was . . . something awkward to him in the normal man-woman relationships in ballet" (144), Ramsay Burt is certain that Ni-

*A more charitable interpretation than Karsavina's is that Nijinsky was replacing conventional mime with the naturalist movement style he learned from Fokine.

jinsky, as Albrecht, was the "good male partner" European audiences had been lacking (74). According to Denby:

> Nijinsky in his pictures is a model of courtesy. The firmness of support he gives his partner is complete. He stands straight enough for two. His expression toward her is intense—in *Giselle* it expresses a supernatural relation, in *Pavillon* one of admiration, in *Faune* one of desire, in *Spectre* one of tenderness—and what a supporting arm that is in *Spectre*, as long and as strong as two. But he observes as well an exact personal remoteness, he shows clearly the fact that they are separate bodies. He makes a drama of their nearness in space. ("Notes" 16)

Kirstein, for a change, was even more adamant about Nijinsky's heterosexuality: "From the photographs we might assume that Albrecht was one of Nijinsky's most glorious roles. His facial expression seems helplessly enraptured, his carriage noble, his balance perfect, his attachment to the ballerina a paroxysm of devotion" (*Nijinsky Dancing* 83). (At least Denby recognized the personal remoteness.)

He meant to say paragon of devotion, of course, not paroxysm. The inadvertently orgasmic figure may be symptomatic of a scandalous anecdote—or fable—Kirstein, elsewhere, tried to repress. Diaghilev did have Nijinsky fired by the Imperial Ballet, which freed him to work for the Ballets Russes alone, by making him refuse to wear the bloomers that had been part of Albrecht's costume since the turn of the century.* Legend has

---

*Nureyev refused to wear them too, but no scandal ensued.

it that Nijinsky also refused to wear a dance belt underneath tights of "golden tissue," offending aristocrats in the audience (Bourman 83). Oddly enough, Kirstein found this story appalling and "mendacious" (*Nijinsky Dancing* 83). Other gays, including Proust, found it fascinating and were especially titillated by the possibility that Nijinsky was undersized, a rumor several Nijinsky biographers attempt to disprove. To quote a Proust biographer:

At the end of January [1911] Nijinsky had danced in *Giselle* wearing an extraordinarily short tunic, designed by Benois and abbreviated by Bakst on the instructions of Diaghilev; and beneath this tunic he had been induced to discard an indispensable article of protective clothing. The Dowager-Empress could scarcely believe what she saw, or thought she saw; and although protocol demanded that she should pretend to have seen nothing, the revelation of Nijinsky's protuberances was taken as a personal insult to the imperial family. He was dismissed immediately. On both sides the incident was a ludicrous but sinister pretext for a final rift. The court circles which controlled the Imperial Ballet were anxious to be rid of Diaghilev, feeling that he had turned the Maryinsky Theatre into a mere winter home for his private troupe; while Diaghilev, conversely, instead of being dependent on the services of dancers on summer leave from the Imperial Ballet, could now organize the Ballets Russes as an independent and permanent company. Proust sent his sympathy to Bakst and "Vestris," as he insisted on nicknaming Nijinsky; but on hearing that the

scandal had been a put-up job he withdrew his good wishes
to the young dancer: "he only interested me as a victim,"
he told Reynaldo [Hahn], "and if he hasn't been victimised,
then" (using his favorite rude word) "*merde* to him."
(Painter 2: 169)

I'm reminded of Nureyev's gay biographer, who was titillated
by the possibility that his subject was oversized.* But I don't
appreciate Proust's reaction. Nijinsky interests me to the extent he wasn't a victim. Unlike gay men invested in the pathos
of his life (Kirstein, who saw Nijinsky's early retirement as an
early death; Proust, who'd have had Nijinsky disowned by the
social class that Proust himself disowned), I see Nijinsky as for-
tunate. He was in the right place at the right time to capitalize
on his talent. And he wouldn't have danced past the age of
twenty-five even if he hadn't lost his mind. Nor do I appreciate
Kirstein's denial of Nijinsky's self-exposure—a mythic flash
point which, I must admit, offers me an imaginary satisfaction
if not a paroxysm of devotion. The denial, however, isn't all
that odd. To cite a second critical commonplace, the phallus
can't afford to be unveiled. Neither, in many circumstances,
can the penis. Of course, gay men—unlike straight men, or so
they say—love to see the penis and imagine the phallus of the
Other even if they aren't very large. Which explains why it was
Kirstein—despite the symptomatic paroxysm—and not Denby

---

*See Stuart: "Handsome, rich, endowed with a gift that, had he opted for
a career in pornography, would have earned him a double-digit nickname [not
'Vestris'], Nureyev was lord of the land and more" (155).

who insisted upon Nijinsky's attachment to the ballerina and concealed the dancer's phallus. Kirstein, having been married to a woman, wandered into and identified with heterosexuality from time to time. Denby, having never been married, stopped at the border.

Unless, of course, the conventional attachment to Karsavina is really rather perverse. On one level, the gendered body language in a classical pas de deux signifies romantic love and heterosexual desire: strong, solid, and stable men guide, support, carry, manipulate, and gaze at women delicately balanced *en pointe*, limbs extended into space. On another level, it signifies something even gayer than the fetishism psychoanalysis posits as central to heterosexual desire. The ballerina can be seen as a "giant dancing phallus, crowned with a tiara" (English 19). The pas de deux can be seen as "male masturbation" (Burt 64). And "the point at which [the ballerina] at last goes limp"—often the moment of death, as in *Giselle*—can be seen as "the orgasm of the phallus . . . she represents in the fantasy of the hero" (English 19). Or at least they can be seen that way on the level of the unconscious, making Nijinsky's partnering blatantly queer, or homoerotic, if he was inept and secretly queer, or autoerotic, if he was adept.

But assuming the accuracy of the anecdote, why did Nijinsky agree to ditch the dance belt? Why, that is, apart from a desire to please Diaghilev and dance in his company? When Jim Morrison showed his penis in concert, he did so because he hated the ideology of cock rock and wanted to prevent us from seeing him as a singing phallus. The exposure, of course, didn't demystify him. The circumstances weren't right and so paroxysmic fans still devote themselves to his Parisian grave—modern-day Albrechts at the tomb of Giselle. You have to give him credit for trying, though. Perhaps Nijinsky had a similar motivation. Perhaps—and this is my imaginary, gender-transitive satisfaction—he was thinking along Morrison's feminist lines and not along his character's prefeminist ones while Karsavina—a woman with whom he did in fact connect, if not in ways she could discern—was telling him to come closer.

Paris, 1910

MUSIC: SINDING

CHOREOGRAPHY: FOKINE

SETS: KOROVINE

COSTUMES: BAKST

❦

Danse siamoise

*I*n the closing divertissement of the second Paris season, Fokine gave Nijinsky a solo that recalled Siamese dancers who'd visited St. Petersburg at the turn of the century. One reason he did so, apart from the popularity of Orientalism, is that Siamese dance, for Fokine, embodied self-expression. It was a perception shared by other members of his circle, including Vasily Rozanov. Writing in a 1901 issue of *Mir iskusstva*, the journal begun by Diaghilev, Rozanov described the dance as natural, meaningful, and fully corporeal—unlike the logocentrism of Western culture and the partial corporeality of classical ballet. Whereas ballet uses only arms and legs, Rozanov argued, Siamese dance uses hands, torso, and face as well. Facial expression, moreover, enhances the "mysterious" presence of the Siamese dancers, who seem to be sleepwalking.

Fokine, however, was equally interested in kinetic self-expression and so made *Danse siamoise* more mobile than the art form it imitated. Not that many noticed. Although Nijinsky emphasized "dominant leg movements, related more to Russian folk dance than to the Siamese ballet, [an exercise in] soft, almost disarticulated, gestures," his audience concentrated on the way he both "communicated an 'oriental presence' through the use of hieratic pose and gesture" (Misler 82) and resembled a "statue of an ancient oriental god in the midst of the empty stage" (Krasovskaya 144). For example, Duncan Grant—a static artist who identified with, designed for, and became ob-

99

sessed with Nijinsky—saw the ballet in static terms as well.*
Grant kept several photographs of *Danse siamoise* in his stu-
dio at Charleston, photographs moreover of Nijinsky semire-
cumbent. In 1925, he based a comic portrait of Lytton Strachey
on one of these photographs. (The comedy relates to a disparity: Strachey being, for Grant, mostly mind; Nijinsky mostly
body.) And in 1972 he based an oil painting on it—titled, stati-
cally enough, *Still Life with Photograph of Nijinsky*.† Kirstein,
however, noticed—or imagined—the kinetic quality of *Danse
siamoise*. "While Fokine may have remembered the quivering
delicacy of Thai fingers," Kirstein wrote shortly after Grant
painted the still life, "Nijinsky's spectacular *entrechat* was
purely virtuosic. It demonstrated again the soaring quality (*ballon*) of his leap, which was as extraordinary as its actual dimensions (*élévation*). The photographs emphasize his intense
concentration, his animal eagerness in realizing expressive pro-
files, his feline propulsion—above all, his exuberance, which
seems all but ecstatic" (*Nijinsky Dancing* 89).

It's hard to reconcile these two orientations: the man who
saw Nijinsky live envisioned him at rest; the man who hadn't
seen Nijinsky live imagined him in motion. Maybe Grant and
Kirstein had divergent sexualities: one static, one kinetic. Or
one with an immobile relation to the Other, one with a mobile

---

*Grant was the Nijinsky of Bloomsbury: a queer little faun coddled by
Vanessa Bell, Lytton Strachey, and John Maynard Keynes.

†Late in life, Grant based other images on photographs of Nijinsky in
Schéhérazade and *Narcisse*. He also made sketches that combined sodomiti-
cal and balletic positions. See Turnbaugh, *Private*.

relation. And maybe mobile, here, is necessarily synonymous with life-affirming, immobile with death-driven. Or maybe not. The opposition stasis/kinesis is inherently unstable. Recall Claudel's observation that even in repose Nijinsky seemed imperceptibly to be dancing. Recall Koestenbaum's fantasy of flying yet not flying into sexual maturity. So when Kirstein fantasized Nijinsky's feline propulsion, he probably imagined crouching cats about to pounce—the Golden Slave just before his entrance. And when he fantasized Nijinsky's all but ecstatic exuberance, he probably imagined men about to have an orgasm—Albrecht just before Giselle saves his life. Men that is on the static verge of bliss, momentarily in between the kinesis of intercourse and the kinesis of ejaculation. Or, making the same point in sublimated terms, men about to express delight facially. In a fantastic description of a painting based on a photograph of *Danse siamoise* in which Nijinsky is upright, Kirstein wrote:

> The big finished oil painting by [Jacques-Emile] Blanche shows Nijinsky standing full-length in his iridescent carapace, glowing in a dark silhouette against the lacquered fold of a Coromandel screen. One hand, fingers close-curved into a simple lotus bud, barely taps his strong high-profiled chin. The other, fingers splayed wide against his chest, seems to echo some plastic manual signal. But beyond any borrowed exotic gesture is Nijinsky's marvelous half-smile, the secret ineffable satisfaction past any self, his bliss is everything sinuous and glistening in some indescribable paradise of dancing. (*Nijinsky Dancing* 89)

Note the connection to Rozanov, who associated the mysterious visage of Siamese dancers with sleepwalking, another semi-static, semikinetic condition. Note too Kirstein's tendency to predicate Nijinsky in terms that suggest both stasis and kinesis: supple, glowing, glistening, sinuous. And note his figuration of Nijinsky's facial expression as a half-smile, indicating once again momentary stasis on the verge of kinetic bliss—to half smile is to be about to smile—and reminding us of Pater's performative description of another famous half-smile and Barthes's description of another famous face.

Pater's description, of which Kirstein was aware, concerns a static image: "[La Gioconda] is older than the rocks among which she sits; like the vampire, she has been dead many times, and learned the secrets of the grave" (Renaissance 130).* Barthes's description, of which Kirstein was unaware, concerns a moving image:

Garbo still belongs to that moment in cinema when capturing the human face still plunged audiences into the

*Van Vechten was aware of the description as well and associated it with both Nijinsky and a blind date. "I remember once, at a performance of the Russian Ballet, I sat in a box next to a most intelligent man, a writer himself; I was meeting him for the first time, and he was seeing the ballet for the first time. [This] indifferent observer became that evening himself a fervent disciple of the Ballet [because] Nijinsky gave him . . . a basis for dreams, for thinking, for poetry. The ennobling effect of all great and perfect art [is] to set our minds wandering in a thousand channels, to suggest new outlets. Pater's experience before the Mona Lisa is unique only in its intense and direct expression" ("Russian Ballet" 12–13).

deepest ecstasy, when one literally lost oneself in a human image as one would in a philtre, when the face represented a kind of absolute state of the flesh, which could be neither reached nor renounced. A few years earlier the face of Valentino was causing suicides; that of Garbo still partakes of the same rule of Courtly Love, where the flesh gives rise to mystical feelings of perdition. (*Mythologies* 56)

This "reminder" is, of course, somewhat facile. I'm a bit too quick to demonize Nijinsky, linking him with two more femmes fatales; too quick to queer both Nijinsky and Kirstein, conflating Kirstein's figuration of a beloved male face with homosexual figurations of beloved female faces; too quick to postmodernize, or poststructuralize, them—always already collapsing the oppositions, including stasis/kineses, upon which any reading of Nijinsky, including Kirstein's, depends and doing so, as a Derridean, to deconstruct, or write off, Western metaphysics altogether. But I don't find the prospect all but ecstatic. I write these lines and write off metaphysics with a rueful half-smile, knowing on one level that the deconstruction won't happen and on another level that I don't want it to. For if it happened, I'd have no way imaginable of understanding Nijinsky— even though the limited understanding I do have is based on concepts, oppositions, and ideologies that are, in fact, more trouble than they're worth.

Paris, 1911

MUSIC: WEBER/BERLIOZ

LIBRETTO: GAUTIER/VAUDOYER

CHOREOGRAPHY: FOKINE

SETS AND COSTUMES: BAKST

Le Spectre de la rose

Nijinsky's most famous leap is the exit through the open window in *Le Spectre de la rose*. Although anticipated, Nijinsky having flown offstage in both *Le Pavillon d'Armide* and *L'Oiseau d'or*, this liberating literalization of gay male flight at the end of a literalization of prancing was simply astonishing. "It was the greatest leap of the century," wrote Denby. "He seemed to the audience to float slowly up like a happy spirit. He seemed to radiate a power of mysterious assurance as calmly as the bloom of a summer rose does." It had, moreover, an "emotional effect [that] can only be described as supernatural, as a strangely beneficent magic." And it approached "those mysterious hints of gentleness that occasionally absorb the human mind" ("Flight" 503, 504). Garafola clarifies Denby's meaning. "A she-man in rose petals," she writes, Nijinsky flouted heterosexual convention: "Masculine in the power of his leaps, feminine in the curving delicacy of his arms, he emitted a perfume of sexual strangeness; he seemed a living incarnation of the third sex, a Uranian reveling in the liberation of his true self" (*Diaghilev* 33).

Feminine arms, masculine legs. Nijinsky's androgyny—indeed, androgyny in general—isn't usually this legible.* Most

---

*See, once again, Barthes's performative description of Greta Garbo: "[She] offered to one's gaze a sort of Platonic Idea of the human creature, which explains why her face is almost sexually undefined, without however leaving one in doubt. It is true that [*Queen Christina*] lends itself to this lack

dance critics, however, agree with Garafola.* Buckle too detected a gender and sexuality division between the Specter's arms and legs. Ending with a Freudian slip—gaze (gays?) for haze—Buckle described the arms as follows:

[Nijinsky] sensed that for a *man* to be dressed in rose petals and to carry on in this giddy non-stop way [a reference to the *enchaînements*], waltzing by himself, as he did at the beginning and end of the ballet, was absurd. That a sexless inhuman being should appear and dance thus was a different matter. He abolished the classical correctness of the *port de bras*, curling his arms round his face and holding them, when extended, with broken wrists and curled-up fingers, so that they became art-noveau tendrils. [And] as he danced the endless dance, hardly coming to rest for a moment, weaving evanescent garlands in the air, his lips were parted in ecstasy and he seemed to emit a perfumed gaze. (178–79)[†]

---

of differentiation; but Garbo does not perform in it any feat of transvestism; she is always herself, and carries without pretence, under her crown or her wide-brimmed hats, the same snowy solitary face" (*Mythologies* 56).

*Denby, in denial, is an exception: "The power of the arms makes their tendrillike bendings as natural as curvings are in a powerful world of young desire; while weaker and more charming arms might suggest an effeminate or saccharine coyness. There is indeed nothing effeminate in these gestures; there is far too much force in them" ("Notes" 17). Cf. Siegel: the Specter of the Rose is "an extension of both the effete prince and the sensuous but not quite real character part" (104).

[†]Sexless, here, means effeminate and homosexual. Cf. Denby: "The Spectre . . . has no age or sex" ("Notes" 19).

Burt detects the division as well, claiming the legs "conformed to conventional expectations of male strength and prowess" (82) and thus demonstrated Nijinsky's phallic mastery.* And even though he'd found the Bluebird's arms and legs equally effeminate, Van Vechten made a similar, synesthetic claim:

> [Nijinsky's dancing in *Le Spectre de la rose*] is the despair of all novices and almost all other virtuosi. After a particularly difficult leap . . . it is a marvel to observe how, without an instant's pause to regain his poise, he rhythmically glides into the succeeding gesture. His dancing has the unbroken quality of music, the balance of great painting, the meaning of fine literature, and the emotion inherent in all these arts. [It is] an imaginative triumph, and the spectator, perhaps, should not be interested in further dissection of it, but a more intimate observer must realize that behind this the effect produced depends on his supreme command of his muscles. ("Russian Ballet" 7)

Nor are critics the only writers to schematize Nijinsky's mysterious assurance this way. Jean Genet does so when describing Darling Daintyfoot, a masterful and masturbatory pimp with a genius for androgyny that approached the dancer's. To quote at length from *Our Lady of the Flowers* (1943), published the year Denby noted the assurance:

*See Burt: "Whereas women [in ballet] are a mystery to be investigated and exposed, men are tested. The evidence suggests that, in these virtuosic roles, Nijinsky passed the test" (82). If so, the mysterious assurance Denby associated with the Specter combines feminine mystery and masculine mastery.

Darling Daintyfoot arrived. There was in his supple bearing the weighty magnificence of the barbarian who tramples choice furs beneath his muddy boots. The torso on his hips was a king on a throne. Merely to have mentioned him is enough for my left hand in my torn pocket to. . . . And the memory of Darling will not leave me until I have completed my gesture. One day the door of my cell opened and framed him. I thought I saw him, in the twinkling of an eye, as solemn as a walking corpse, set in the thickness—which you can only imagine—of the prison walls. He appeared standing before me with the same graciousness that might have been his lying naked in a field of pinks. I was his at once, as if (who said that?) he had discharged through my mouth straight to my heart. Entering me until there was no room left for myself, so that now I am one with gangsters, burglars, and pimps, and the police arrest me by mistake. For three months he regaled himself with my body, beating me for all he was worth. I dragged at his feet, more trampled on than a dust mop. Ever since he has gone off free to his robberies, I keep remembering his gestures, so vivid they revealed him cut out of a faceted crystal, gestures so vivid that you suspected they were all involuntary, for it seems utterly impossible that they were born of ponderous reflection and decision. Of the tangible him there remains, sad to say, only the plaster cast that Divine herself made of his cock, which was gigantic when erect. The most impressive thing about it is the vigor, hence the beauty, of that part which goes from the anus to the tip of the penis.

I shall say that he had lace fingers, that, each time he awoke, his outstretched arms, open to receive the World, made him look like the Christ Child in his manger—with the heel of one foot on the instep of the other—that his eager face offered itself, as it bent backward facing heaven, that, when standing, he would tend to make the basket movement we see Nijinsky making in the old photos where he is dressed in shredded roses. His wrist, fluid as a violinist's, hangs down, graceful and loose-jointed. And at times, in broad daylight, he strangles himself with his lithe arm, the arm of a tragedienne.

This is almost an exact portrait of Darling, for . . . he had a talent for the gesture that thrills me, and, if I think about him, I can't stop praising him until my hand is smeared with my liberated pleasure. (59–61, first ellipsis in original)

But if Nijinsky's "spectacular jump" made him "appear strong" (Burt 56), what then? The rarely seen aftermath of the leap—Nijinsky is said to have been so exhausted by the maneuver as to have landed either on a mattress or in the arms of his valet—is almost as mythic as the leap itself. And both versions of the aftermath, being tainted with weakness, are tinged with gayness. Buckle presented the first version via Valentine Gross, a second static artist obsessed with Nijinsky, who found Nijinsky "quite alone, curled up on the floor, panting, like a bird fallen from a nest. His hands were clutched over his heart, which she could hear beating in spite of the distant roar of applause" (305). Gross herself noted that Nijinsky "was like a

crumpled rose in pain": "I was so touched that I left him alone and said nothing. Then he saw me and sprang up like a child taken by surprise and came smiling towards me. As he stood beside me in his leotard sewn with damp purplish petals, he seemed a kind of St. Sebastian, flayed alive and bleeding from innumerable wounds" (quoted in Buckle 305). This inverts accounts that picture Karsavina, the young lady who dreams the ballet, as Nijinsky's victim, as the subject of another rape fantasy.* But it jibes with homoerotic accounts of tragic early death that feature Sebastian, including one starring Rubinstein—even if those accounts aren't so ignorant as to have the saint flayed alive. (Sebastian, a gay martyr, succumbed to a fusillade of arrows; Marsyas, a musical one, was flayed alive for having failed to compete with Apollo.)

Cocteau presented the second version of the aftermath. In a contemporary caricature Burt misreads as a confirmation of the strength required by the leap, he pictured Nijinsky after the exit, collapsed on a chair, cradled by his valet (Vasili), fanned by his masseur (Dmitri), and surrounded by Diaghilev, Bakst, José Sert, and Serge Grigoriev, the company's *régisseur*. The impression the caricature creates isn't exactly phallic.† Nor is the

---

*According to Cocteau, "After he has bid a last farewell to his beloved victim, he evaporates through the window in a jump so poignant, so contrary to all the laws of flight and balance, following so high and curved a trajectory, that I shall never again smell a rose without this ineffable phantom appearing before me" (*Comoedia illustré*, June 15, 1911).

†I do, however, get a phallic impression from Cocteau's verbal—and retrospective—accounts of the aftermath: "After kissing the girl, the Spectre of the Rose leaps out her window . . . and lands among the stagehands, who squirt water into his face and scrub at him with towels, like a boxer between rounds. What grace coupled with what brutality! I still hear the thunder of that applause, still see that young man smeared with greasepaint, sweating, panting, one hand pressing his heart and the other clutching a stage brace. He collapsed on a chair, and in a few seconds, slapped, drenched, pummeled, he walked back out onstage, bowing, smiling" (quoted in Phelps 49). Or again: "He invented a double leap, by which he curled up in the air backstage and fell perpendicularly" (Cocteau, *Journals* 54).

impression it creates detumescent. Nijinsky, here, looks like a woman in a swoon, surrounded by more or less imaginary lovers. Think Emma Bovary or Blanche DuBois. If weakness in Gross's verbal version of the aftermath connotes homosexuality (a mythic indication, for Barthes), weakness in Cocteau's visual version denotes it (a linguistic indication)—indications which do, after all, relate to the uncloseted liberation movement of leaping out a window.

In *Spectre of the Rose* (1946), a film that anticipates *The Red Shoes* (1948), Ivan Kirov plays André Sannine, a conventionally masculine and unconventionally heterosexual dancer meant to be read as Nijinsky. Sannine, like Nijinsky, is insane. He recreates Nijinsky's roles—Harlequin, the Golden Slave, Petrouchka, the Faun, and the Specter of the Rose—in macho costumes and manly movements. (No effeminate arm motion for Sannine.) And he truly victimizes women who recreate Karsavina's, murdering them. The first time Sannine attempts Nijinsky's leap, in performance, we see him land. (So much for literalizing—and straightening—the figure of gay male flight; apparently, Sannine never saw *The Thief of Baghdad*.) The second time he attempts it, in reality although he's wearing his rose costume, we neither see him land nor imagine a version of Nijinsky's aftermath. Instead, we picture Sannine plastered against the pavement because he's leapt, or crashed, through his closed apartment window—something only madmen and weaklings do, not something only gay men do.* Twentieth-century tragic early death

---

*Suicide isn't a female malady anymore. Nor is it now considered courageous.

may be primarily homoerotic, but purportedly straight men still elicit sentimental responses by killing themselves.

Gay reenactments of *Le Spectre de la rose*, however, have survived Sannine's first weakness: the visible landing. Gays have remained liberated and, unlike Nijinsky, sane even though they haven't really flown. Some of us, that is, aren't intimidated by mastery we can't attain—and so Van Vechten was wrong to characterize Nijinsky's dancing as the despair of all other novices and virtuosi. Serge Lifar, the Marsyas to whom Massine passed Diaghilev along, may have been too intimidated to attempt the final exit but George de la Pena isn't.* Pena recreates the role beautifully in *Nijinsky* (1980), including the effeminate arm motion and, with the help of trick photography, repeating the unrepeatable exit. And Duncan Grant—even knowing no one thought he was about to take off and never telling himself, as Apollonian Denby did, to hold the pose—used to imitate the leap with Dionysian "verve" (Jacobs 16). How so? Perhaps, like Barthes, Grant satisfied himself by imagining his imitation to be virtuosic. According to Barthes, a complaisant pianist:

> If I play badly—aside from the lack of velocity, which is a
> purely muscular problem—it is because I fail to abide by

*See Kirstein: "Serge Lifar, costumed and made up identically to Nijinsky, appeared in his version of Fokine's *Spectre de la rose* . . . an adequate archaeological reconstruction of lost visual aspects, but soulless as far as dancing was concerned; the final legendary leap through the window was not even attempted. If I had been ignorant of what it represented, it would probably not have interested me at all. As Romola Nijinsky said, 'jumps or no jumps, it was all unrepeatable'" (*Mosaic* 230).

the written fingering: I improvise, each time I play, the position of my fingers, and therefore I can never play anything without making mistakes. The reason for this is obviously that I want an immediate pleasure and reject the tedium of training, for training hampers pleasure—for the sake of a greater ulterior pleasure, as they say (we tell the pianist what the gods said to Orpheus: Don't turn back *prematurely* on the effects of your action). So that the piece, in the perfection attributed to it but never really attained, functions as a bit of a hallucination: I gladly give myself up to the watchword of a fantasy: *"Immediately!"* even at the cost of a considerable loss of reality. (*Roland Barthes* 70)

Or perhaps, putting *amour propre* back into amateurism, Grant felt compelled neither to compete nor to hallucinate—which is the self-affirming, self-accepting leap of faith with which this section should end. Yet I feel compelled, for reasons you might imagine, to close by quoting the astonishing and heartrending projection of a Nijinsky admirer with fewer lovers than either Nijinsky, Grant, or Barthes. According to Charles Ricketts, who never imitated the Specter of the Rose, "Nijinsky never once touched the ground, but laughed at our sorrows and passions in mid-air" (174–75).

Paris, 1911

MUSIC: TCHEREPNIN

LIBRETTO: BAKST

CHOREOGRAPHY: FOKINE

SETS AND COSTUMES: BAKST

Narcisse

*W*e saw streams, boulders, meadows, willow trees, scudding clouds, and blue sky. We saw Echo (Karsavina) but not Ganymede. We then saw Narcissus (Nijinsky) leap onstage. Oskar Kokoschka, writing to Romola Nijinsky, was mesmerized by the entrance. "Onstage, among a group of costumed male dancers, there suddenly appeared a Being—wholly effortless, wholly innocent of acquired momentum; he rose, he floated on air in defiance of the law of gravity, before disappearing again into the scenery. Here was a secret which I could not understand, but have never forgotten" (quoted in Néagu 44). Prince Peter Lieven, however, wasn't. "Nijinsky's entrance was a failure. He appeared on the stage with a positively tremendous leap, and the tense strain of this almost record-breaking jump destroyed the impression of airiness and freedom upon which mainly depended the illusion of Nijinsky's *élévation*. Also the crash of his landing, almost in the centre of the stage, was heard throughout the entire house and made a bad impression" (154–55).

Impressions differ. Narcissus self-divides. Kokoschka's dancer defies gravity; Lieven's succumbs to it, anticipating his assymetrical exit or final plunge. But Narcissus is always already riven. The mythic figure, choosing between Ganymede and Echo, selects himself.* The modern figure, choosing be-

---

*A pregay narcissism: he's rejected both homosexuality and heterosexuality. The ballet, having jettisoned Ganymede and invoked the psychoanalytic equation of same-sex and self-same, homoeroticizes narcissism.

tween stasis and kinesis, selects both—and this time people noticed. Van Vechten saw Nijinsky as more mobile than Benois, for one, had imagined possible.* "Nijinsky not only did some very beautiful dancing," he wrote, "but posed (as the Greek youth who admired himself in the mirror of the pool) with such utter and arresting grace that even here he awakened a new kind of emotion" ("Russian Ballet" 10).† Kirstein noticed—or imagined—it too: "He stares into his pool and sees the youth there who echoes to perfection his own dazzling variety of steps and poses" (*Nijinsky Dancing* 123). (So much for the opposition of static and kinetic sexualities.) Narcissus self-divides along gender lines as well. Many nineteenth-century ballets (*La Sylphide* [1832], *Giselle* [1841], *Coppélia* [1870], *Swan Lake* [1896]) concern the impossible love of mortal or unworthy men for enchanted, unattainable women. *Narcisse*, upsetting this ideology, concerns both the impossible love of an enchanted

---

*Benois, at first, considered Narcissus too static for ballet: "fixed as a statue, [he'd] stare himself into drowning" (quoted in Kirstein, *Nijinsky Dancing* 123).

†Or not so new. Narcissus aroused classy heterosexuals other than Echo and classical homosexuals other than Ganymede. Ricketts found that "Duchesses had to be led out of the audience, blinded with emotion, and with their diamond tiaras all awry" (79). Kokoschka, upon close inspection, found Nijinsky's upper body to be "as graceful as that of an *ephebe*" and his lower body to be as powerful as a horse. "I deliberately dropped my napkin," he told a woman who wouldn't have allowed the dinner-table trespass, "and in retrieving it touched his thigh; I could well believe that it belonged to a centaur rather than a man, for he had muscles of steel. But even that fell short of explaining the hidden essence of his being; it did not unravel the secret" (quoted in Néagu 44).

woman (Echo) for a mortal man and the impossible love of a mortal man for "himself."* Nijinsky, then, reenacted a conventional male role (Siegfried in *Swan Lake*) as well as an unconventional female role (Echo in *Narcisse*). His body, however, wasn't riven sexually. The graceful arms and powerful legs, unlike those of the Specter of the Rose, moved as one. Denby, then, was right to claim, "In the Narcissus pose the savage force of the arms and legs makes credible that the hero's narcism was not vanity, but an instinct that killed him, like an act of God" ("Notes" 17).

Or nearly right. Denby, here, should have equated the arms and legs but shouldn't have insisted upon their savage force.† Once again, he was concerned to eliminate the taint of both effeminacy and homosexuality. Indeed, he was even more concerned to do so than in connection with *Le Spectre de la rose* because the loaded charge of gay narcissism was now in play. Hence the typo: "narcism" for narcissism. Denby literally if accidentally erased narcissism, or enough of the word to undermine its meaning. It's a slip I can appreciate. For if Denby's vir-

---

*I use quotation marks because any version of the myth contends with the fact that the self Narcissus sees reflected is an ideal, or alien, Other—a contention embedded in Kirstein's figure: "the youth there . . . *echoes to perfection* his . . . steps and poses."

†No other critic uses such terminology, although Bronislava Nijinska (Nijinsky's sister) came close. "His body of the youth in love with his own image emanated health and the athletic prowess of the ancient Greek Games. It could have been dangerous to portray in a dance the sensual and erotic Narcisse, driven to ecstasy by his own reflection in the water. Vaslav had so interpreted this scene that all such implications disappeared, dissolved in the beauty of his dance" (366).

ilization of Nijinsky was misguided and possibly misogynistic, his de-vanitization of Nijinsky's tragic early death in *Narcisse*, even though essentialist and irresponsible ("an instinct . . . killed him, like an act of God"), was a welcome challenge to the modern tendency to associate homosexuality with self-love. (As if heterosexuality weren't narcissistic. Look in a mirror, Freud and Lacan.)

Now about that tragic, or not so tragic, early death. *Narcisse* represents Nijinsky's second such demise. But whereas the Golden Slave is killed, an execution complicated by the character's *jouissance*, Narcissus kills himself, a suicide complicated by the fact that it's an accident. Gays reacted to this apolitically—because the narrative, unlike *Schéhérazade*, features neither societal nor internalized homophobia. We reacted to it nonsentimentally—due to the lack of both homophobia and suicidal agency.* And we reacted rather placidly. To quote Beaumont, "crouched by the edge of the pool, he gazed spellbound at his own image, bending down with infinite grace closer and closer to the water, until he disappeared beneath its surface" (38). The beloved had barely left—or sunk beneath—the stage before we mourned, or thought we mourned, his loss and turned our devoted attention to the flower that took his place. We heard the ululations of the chorus, we saw Echo weep as she too disappeared into the scenery (a far cry from the Sultan's tears), yet we were unmoved.

The Picture of Dorian Gray is worth considering here. In it, another self-involved ephebe accidentally kills himself by colliding with a mirror image—much to the gothic horror if not the antihomophobic chagrin of Wilde's gay readers.

Some of us, however, are moved by Nijinsky's narcissism in ways that actually get us somewhere—if only in our imaginations.* But as Kirstein came to realize with the help of the Fontainebleau farandole, imaginative adventure can result in real adventure. At ten, Kirstein studied dance with an "Isadorable" who "obliterated all my self-doubts about sissiness" (*Mosaic* 38)—one reason to let queer boys learn ballet. Shortly thereafter, having studied Nijinsky's own talent and tragedy (the early retirement) without having seen *Narcisse*, Kirstein came to see theatrical narcissism (the "more or less controlled" [Apollonian yet Dionysian] employment of hysteria and self-obsession) as the "*sine qua non* of memorable . . . execution," as the way to make oneself "more extraordinary [than is] God-given," and as the key to a Paterian "quest for emotion for its own sake" (*Mosaic* 77)—all three of which he associates with self-expression. Then again, many people—gay or not, Freudian or not, Lacanian or not—associate identification with misrecognition and self-expression with misrepresentation. I, for one, insist that my own narcissism is merely performative, or theatrical, yet feel most myself when pretending to be less intelligent and attractive than I really am—a pretension typical, it would appear, of Petrouchka.

*Mourning is kinetic. Sentimental self-indulgence or melancholy, a form of sentimentality I no longer abide, is static.

Paris, 1911

MUSIC: STRAVINSKY

LIBRETTO: STRAVINSKY/BENOIS

CHOREOGRAPHY: FOKINE

SETS AND COSTUMES: BENOIS

✤

Petrouchka

Nijinsky's two deaths in *Petrouchka* defy interpretation, a fact reflected in more than one description. To quote Buckle:

> [Petrushka] shoots from the booth, running on tip-toe, hands clasped between his legs, with the armed Moor in hot pursuit. The Ballerina has her hands over her ears in terror as Petrushka is struck down. The crowd gathers round to watch his brief death scene, hear his last pathetic piping cry, watch his final gesture of appeal. A watchman goes to fetch the Magician, who appears, top-hatted this time, from a refreshment stall. There are a few threatening gestures from the crowd. The Magician lifts the limp puppet which has by now replaced Nijinsky . . . and shakes it to show it is nothing but wood and sawdust. The crowd disperses and the pumping accordions again emphasize the bleakness of the winter night. The Magician, left alone, passes slowly across to the left of the stage, dragging the puppet. Suddenly Petrushka's squeaking fanfare is heard and Nijinsky as the puppet's ghost appears menacing over the booth where he learned sorrow, with "frantic waving arms." Has his soul survived? The terrified Magician slinks off, the ghost of Petrushka falls forward and hangs with swinging arms over the top of the booth, and the music ends with a curious question-mark on the plucked strings. (197)

What can it mean, and what can it mean for gay men, that Petrouchka became a "ghost," that his ghost died, and that it was moving when the curtain fell?

One reason the deaths defy interpretation is that Petrouchka himself is almost unreadable. He's a complicated combination of the Russian Punch and the French Pierrot, or of victimizer and victim.* And Pierrot alone, around the turn of the century, is complicated enough: flighty, frenetic, and superficial as of old, yet newly anguished, melancholy, and narcissistic. The term sad clown, in other words, doesn't even begin to describe him, for he's both Hamlet and Pagliacci—something homoerotic literati had known for quite some time. Théophile Gautier, anticipating Nijinsky's sense of Petrouchka's alienation, had perceived the synthesis as early as 1847.† "Wan, lanky, dressed in his pale costume, always hungry and always beaten," he wrote, Pierrot is "the pariah, the passive and disinherited being who assists, with gloomy cunning, at the orgies and follies of his masters" (*La Presse*, Jan. 25, 1847). Verlaine, anticipating both the alienation and Nijinsky's embodiment of the second death in a sonnet written shortly before he met Rimbaud ("Pierrot" [1868]), perceived it as well:

This is no longer the lunar dreamer of the old song
Who laughed at his ancestors at the top of the door;

*Punch is sadistic, violent, aggressive, and wicked—a character who beats his wife, murders his neighbors, and goes to hell.

†Petrouchka, Nijinsky told Lady Ottoline Morrell, is "the mythical outcast . . . who beats his hands against the walls, but always is cheated and despised and left outside alone" (Morrell 215).

His gaiety, like his candle, alas! is dead,

And his specter haunts us today, thin and luminous.

And so it is that amidst the terror of a long flash
    of lightning,

His pale blouse has the aspect, in the cold wind that
    carries it away,

Of a winding sheet; and his mouth is gaping, so

That he seems to scream under the gnawings of the worm.

With the sound of a passing flock of night birds,

His white sleeves make vaguely through space

Mad signs to which no one responds,

His eyes are two great holes where phosphorus creeps,

And his flour renders more frightful still

His bloodless face with its pinched nose of one near death.

                          (Storey 238)*

Yet shortly after he left Lucien Létinois, the youth who took Rimbaud's place, Verlaine wrote a poem ("Pierrot gamin" [1886]) that underscores the old-fashioned independence of a newly adolescent figure:

Although hardly any taller than a yardstick,

The roguish little devil knows how to put

The steely glint in his eyes

That suits the subtle genius

Of his infinite malice

As a grimacing poet-charlatan.

*This translation and that of "Pierrot gamin" are by Robert Storey. See Verlaine, *Oeuvres poétiques*, 320–21, 520.

With lips as red as a wound
On which lasciviousness sleeps,
A pale face lit by cunning grins,
Long, its features very sharp,
Accustomed (one might say)
To contemplating every outcome;

A body slim but not scrawny,
A voice girlish but not shrill
—The body of a young ephebe in miniature,
A head voice, a body on holiday—
A creature always ready
To slake every appetite.

(Storey 248)

Verlaine's descriptions of Rimbaud and Létinois—the former "a big bony body that seemed to betray the clumsiness of an adolescent boy who was still growing," the latter "a lanky Pierrot on fatigue-duty" (*Oeuvres en prose* 974, 451)—are worth mentioning here. They suggest the pederastic pretext of both Verlaine's verse and Diaghilev's—or Nijinsky's—Petrouchka.[*] Robert Storey's gloss on the 1868 sonnet is worth mentioning as well: "Now signalling hopelessly to the Other across empty space ['His white sleeves make vaguely through space / Mad signs to which no one responds'], Pierrot has fallen into a world

---

[*]See Beaumont: "[Nijinsky] seemed to have probed the very soul of the character with astonishing intuition. Did he, in one of his dark moods of introspection, feel conscious of a strange parallel between Petrouchka and himself, and the Showman and Diaghilev?" (45).

of human coordinates, of social space and psychic duration, having relinquished the self-determining gestures of the gayer 'Pantomine'" (238). No sooner does Pierrot, now pubescent, become human than his body language becomes senseless. Some Pierrot-lovers took this senselessness to an extreme. For the *Cercle funambulesque* (1888–98)—a group that infused the pantomime with symbolist poetry and drama, or Mallarmé and Maeterlinck—"the mime certain of pleasing the public is the one whose . . . gestures [are] restrained, hardly perceptible, but extraordinarily suggestive!" (Galipaux 104).* Others however, including Michel Carré *fils*, a popular Pierrot at the time, renounced symbolist senseleness. And not only did they renounce symbolism, they renounced humor and irony as well—sentimentalizing and melodramatizing a figure people had been finding hysterical, if not schizophrenic, for over a hundred years.

This then is where Petrouchka entered. On the one hand, an old hand: comic, flighty, knowing, frenetic, superficial, provocative, infantile, insane—and immortal. On the other hand, a new hand: tragic, anguished, naive, melancholy, narcissistic, evocative, adolescent, sane—and doomed.† And in Nijinsky's black-

---

*Storey, for one, claims to understand the suggestive Pierrot of symbolist poetry. That Pierrot, he writes, reiterating Buckle's "ghost," lived "only to die—or to be etherealized into an ideal 'soul' refined of animal appetite" and etiolated "into pure spectrality" (297, 292n).

†See Storey: "Once the depths of 'tragic' expression had been fathomed the lunatic mask could be laid aside" (311). And after Séverin's pantomime *Pauvre Pierrot* (1891), the figure "could suffer and even die, like every human being" (Séverin 179).

mittened hands, Pierrot became even more anomalous.* Not only did Nijinsky straddle melodrama and symbolism, he straddled naturalism (the fair, the crowds) and supernaturalism (the Magician, the puppets) as well. "A puppet with a soul," he straddled humanity and inhumanity.† He straddled extroversion and introversion. He straddled psyche and soma, mind and body. He was a Dostoevskian idiot yet a brilliant artist. He was young and beautiful, or adolescent, yet grotesquely old and unattractive. To quote Kirstein, "Petrouchka is a rueful, poor, ugly, self-pitying Slav Pierrot, clownishly whitefaced and wretched against his rival, a stolid, hot-blooded, rich, blackfaced hussar in green and gold" (*Nijinsky Dancing* 107).

This then is where Petrouchka exits in the fourth and final scene.‡ Comic/tragic, flighty/anguished, knowing/naive, frenetic/melancholy, provocative/evocative, sane/insane, mortal/immortal, human/inhuman, introverted/extroverted, idiotic/brilliant, superficial, narcissistic, infantile, adolescent, and all too adult. But why is Petrouchka melancholy, as opposed to

*Many subsequent Petrouchka's have been white-mittened, much to Denby's chagrin. Still integrating Nijinsky's body, he wrote that "the new costume makes the dance against the black wall in the second scene a foolish hand dance, instead of a dance of a whole figure, as intended" ("Notes" 19).

†For Benois, "the great difficulty of Petrushka's part is to express his pitiful oppression and his hopeless efforts to achieve personal dignity *without ceasing to be a puppet*" (337–38, emphasis original).

‡Kirstein, with respect to the exit in the second scene, wrote that "Petrouchka beats himself pitifully against his paper walls, hurling himself through to a worthless freedom" (*Nijinsky Dancing* 107). No gay liberation there.

mournful?* And why are his two deaths, if they are deaths, tragic? Petrouchka is in love with a Ballerina (Karsavina) who won't give him the time of day, an erotic frustration that represents the "sublime and impossible passion" of many modern Pierrots (Storey 304). But he's also in love with, or homosocially attracted to, the Moor—his murderous rival and alter ego. By the end of the nineteenth century, the homoeroticism implicit in heterosexual desire—the vexed relation of men vis-à-vis the women who come between them, as the Ballerina comes between the two in their pas de trois—became untenable for many straight men, giving Petrouchka yet another impossible passion to contend with and the Moor, a panic-stricken love object who looks like the Golden Slave, homophobic cause to kill him. This, we now know, needn't be the tragic outcome of the ballet. But at the time, one of them did have to die. Had Petrouchka the wherewithal of the Sultan in *Schéhérazade*, for example, he would have murdered the Moor.† All of which renders Petrouchka not only tragic but, at long last, perverse. Then again, Pierrot should have been enacting *primal* perversion all along, according to lovers outside the inner *cercle*. To quote Catulle Mendès (Gautier's son-in-law):

> We have transformed into the poetic, subtle, even perverse Gille of Watteau, the popular Pierrot, the true Pierrot . . .

*Petrouchka is the height of "desolating melancholy," according to *Le Figaro* (June 17, 1911).

†A similar dynamic can be found in E. M. Forster's "The Other Boat" (1915–16) and "The Life to Come" (1922), contemporary fantasies concerning same-sex interracial love.

who, ingenuously and brutally, being an embodiment of childish instinct served by virile strength, having no knowledge of the over-subtle soul, flings himself without premeditation and without remorse, without cleverness or conscience, toward all the satisfactions, even should they lead him through crime. . . . For he is desiring—and incomprehending—Instinct. (240–41)

Without conscience—desiring instinct. Pierrot/Petrouchka, although perverse, is no longer queer, because the unconscious doesn't recognize gender difference. Consciousness does—a tragedy for all of us, as well as for Petrouchka. But no 1911 audience would have accepted a comic ending: Petrouchka and the Moor getting it together and getting it on, let alone Petrouchka, the Moor, and the Ballerina doing so. Nor would many audiences today. Even if she didn't position herself as the proverbial meat in the sandwich, were the Ballerina in my imaginary reconstruction to involve herself in that ménage à or pas de trois, even I might write her off as a "fag hag." (Vanessa Bell in between Duncan Grant and John Maynard Keynes; Lady Ottoline Morrell in between Keynes and Nijinsky.) For most of us, myself included, have yet to become very queer—or to become as queer as Charles Henri Ford and Parker Tyler, prescient lovers and precocious collaborators who in *The Young and Evil* (1933), a brilliant novel that should be rescued from obscurity, imagine Theodosia, the fag-hag character, and neither gay protagonist to occupy first the Ballerina's life-affirming and then Petrouchka's death-driven positions—a function, no doubt, of the impossible passion the men imagine this bisexual woman to have in relation to themselves, but a function of the gender trouble they'd introduce within the ballet as well. To quote Theodosia's fag-hag fantasy, in which she recounts a dream:

I remembered dancing to Chopin's music in silver and starlight with a tragic Pierrot on whose lips were lies but whose dancing was swift music. I remembered [eyes] of men I loved. I remembered [girls'] lips kissing me. . . . But now I have lived too close to death to care for anything: if that were so certain that you could not say the word before others for fear that they might misunderstand and pity you, if you had to keep yourself just so, and sensitised for the death that is taking you and, weak as the body is, to above this wear a personality and talk with people, then would you not perhaps, having been born strange and having lived too much, would you not gently despise the world, and would you not if you had met someone you loved (love being all tangled with the dream of desire), being young in some dim corner where death hadn't invaded yet, and if that person would give nothing of his life, and if he did not desire you, then, my dear, if you had so little of physical strength, would you want it to go out in hopeless hunger, would you not earnestly implore him not to come back, would you not have written everything to him, that he would not come back. (94–95)

Well, you might not have. You might not have implored him not to come back, even knowing he—or she—didn't desire you, even knowing you were dying. Or you might not if you were Petrouchka, which for Ford, Parker, and other queer men may have been the only sensible interpretation of the first element of the ghost's death: the frantic waving arms. "I defy you to manipulate me," said to the Magician. "I defy you to kill me," said to the Moor. "I defy you not to love me," said to the Ballerina—and the Moor. As for the second, final element—the melancholy swinging arms—it may have meant: "You may kill me, but you won't get over me." In the end, Petrouchka is in fact an outcast, left outside and alone—as are we who identify with him. And to quote Wilde, another modern Pierrot, "outcasts always mourn" ("Reading Gaol" 857). We never imagine the dead are gone. We never imagine them at rest. And we never accept substitutes. After all, there'll never be another Wilde. Nor another Nijinsky.

London, 1911

MUSIC: TCHAIKOVSKY

LIBRETTO: BEGICHEV/GELTZER/PETIPA

CHOREOGRAPHY: PETIPA/IVANOV/FOKINE

SETS AND COSTUMES: KOROVINE/GOLOVINE

❧

Le Lac des cygnes

(SWAN LAKE)

Once again, impressions differ. Beaumont, as usual, was enthusiastic:

> The Prince [Siegfried], attended by his friend, entered the glade. Nijinsky wore doublet and hose; on his head was a cap decorated with a long feather. The costume was entirely black except for the hose, which were relieved with vertical pink stripes. Nijinsky's slanting eyes and pale make-up, made paler still in contrast with his dark clothes, gave him a mystic air, the appearance of a man haunted by a vision which he yearns to see again. As he walked near the lake, peering up at the tree-tops or gazing towards the placid water, he made you aware of the presence of mist by the contraction and dilation of his nostrils, and by an almost imperceptible groping movement of his hands, as though he were brushing the mist aside. (31)

A. E. Johnson was less enthusiastic and, in a report more attuned to Karsavina's deprecation of Nijinsky's acting in *Giselle* than to Beaumont's affirmation of the *Sylphides*-like gesture with which Nijinsky seemed to be gazing both retrospectively and prospectively, wrote: "The ballet presents Nijinsky in the kind of role more definitely associated with Adolf Bolm. . . . Nijinsky [is] a dancer who seems almost ill at ease when constrained to limit his movements to the actor's pedestrian paces" (226–33).

Oddly enough, no one complained about Nijinsky's dancing

here, even though the music that accompanied his most important solo raised, in retrospect, a few eyebrows. "The music," wrote Buckle, "was taken by Diaghilev from 'Cassenoisette.' It was the Sugar Plum Fairy's tinkling tune with the celesta; and it is hard to imagine the dance which could have been arranged to this essentially feminine music. Nothing, indeed, could be more out of keeping with the fey character of the lovesick Prince which it seems Nijinsky was trying to create" (218). Notwithstanding that feminine music does sound fey, Buckle's failure of imagination appears to have been contagious, infecting gay choreographers otherwise amenable to causing gender trouble. "I asked three choreographers at dinner one night if they could imagine a man's dance to this music," Buckle added. "[Frederick] Ashton, [John] Taras and Nureyev all replied that they couldn't" (218n). Even Mark Morris, who in *The Hard Nut* (1991) has two men do the most important pas de deux, assigns the Sugar Plum Fairy music along with conventionally feminine choreography to Marie. The problem may not be the music per se, but that it belongs to a fairy. This would account for the tendency of the Nijinsky fans who wrote about his role in *Swan Lake* to focus on the acting rather than the dancing. Whereas Nijinsky's dancing seemed effeminate (yet insufficiently fey) in the solo, his acting, although inept, seemed masculine, representing a man in love with an enchanted woman. It would also account for the similar tendency of the fans who envisioned Nijinsky's Siegfried. In George Barbier's Beardsleyesque and rather fantastic illustration, Nijinsky looks the way Beaumont describes him: brushing mist aside, gazing backward and gesturing forward as if haunted by a vision he yearns to see again. A vision, no doubt, of Swan Maidens—although the birds in the illustration are doves.

It's an arresting and arrested image, not only because Nijinsky seems caught in between the past and the future but because for some reason, despite the heteroeroticism of his yearning, he seems fey as well. This would explain the inclusion—alongside Michelangelo's *David*—of this illustration in *The Gay Pillow Book* (1995). The drawing, the second in a series of twelve Barbier devoted to Nijinsky, is simply the feyest or gayest of the lot. Incidentally, pillow books—erotic manuals exchanged by lovers—have been around a long time. They originated in ancient China and became known as such in medieval Japan, after the wooden pillows in which they were kept. Gay pillow books, of course, are relatively modern, as is gay sexuality, and relatively rare. Another one, Barry Gifford's *Landscape with Traveler: The Pillow Book of Francis Reeves* (1980), is based on and relatively faithful to autobiographical letters written to the author by M.C., balletomane, danseur manqué, and Gifford's dedicatee.* The only aspects of M.C.'s love life Gifford does misrepresent concern the attention Francis Reeves devotes to his sexual history—M.C. considers the attention undue—and the affection he has for Jim, a character Gifford based on himself.† Like M.C., Francis Reeves is queer. "A happy,

---

*Gifford initially wanted to name Francis Reeves "Humbert Humbert," a sign, I'm told by M.C., of his interest in Nabokov. M.C. isn't, in fact, a pedophile—except perhaps in Gifford's imagination.

†M.C. claims he's never been in love with Gifford. Given the frequency with which straight men, unattractive ones in particular, imagine gays find them irresistable, I find the claim credible.

healthy, open-minded, curious bisexuality is the natural state of man," he writes. "Why doesn't the world just relax!" (81). Like M.C., he began studying ballet at twenty-two, under Leon Fokine (Michel's son). Like M.C. and Bersani, but unlike Bill Watson, he dislikes theatrically effeminate behavior.

> Sad, too, to look at the beautiful young men and have their beauty almost totally cancelled out by their theatrically effeminate mannerisms. They were all smoking like Bette Davis, calling each other 'Dahling' like Tallulah, holding their eyelids half-shut like Dietrich—etc., etc., but even that wasn't consistent. It alternated with limp-wristed slaps and playful shoves and high-pitched squeals of 'Oh *Mary*, you bitch, you're really *such* a camp!' and the inevitable sidelong glances to make sure it was not lost on the spectators. (2)

And like M.C., he especially dislikes theatrically effeminate dance. "My great idol in ballet," Francis Reeves writes, "was always [Igor] Youskevitch"—not Nijinsky.

> I used to pray that I'd wake up one morning not only dancing but looking like him. He had (and still has) one of those wonderful, bony, sunken-cheeked Slavic faces, almost ugly, really, which I found most compelling. Besides which, he was the greatest dancer I ever saw. Most male dancers, straight or gay, seem to find it difficult to appear masculine onstage. Even [André] Eglevsky, who was a huge hunk of a man and totally straight (so far as I know), couldn't resist flipping his wrists. But not so Youskevitch. He oozed

masculinity, and when he was onstage you smelled balls! And not perfumed balls, either. (51)

Ned Rorem might suggest that this distaste for the kind of effeminate behavior Nijinsky had to display in *Swan Lake* and Barbier happened to display in the drawing goes hand in hand with the character's distaste for French culture. Francis Reeves calls the French "the only people I know whom it's possible to love and cordially detest at the same time" (118), a sentiment Rorem associates with a preference for Teutonic masculinity and, possibly, heterosexuality: "*Everything* is either French or German. Blue is French, red is German. No is French, yes is German. Cats are French, dogs are German. Night is French, day is German. Women are French, men are German. . . . Gay is French, straight is German (unless it's the other way around). . . . If all this is true—and it *is* (you disagree? you're German)—then I fall roundly into the French category" (24). M.C., however, having been asked to justify himself by someone who finds him fey but not misogynistic (the epithet I hurl at Denby for having denied Nijinsky's effeminate behavior) says he hates German culture even more than Francis Reeves hates French: "French and the other Romance languages, especially Italian, attracted me first. German and the Germans have never done so" (personal communication). He also describes his memories of Nijinsky and attitudes toward effeminate dance.

> When I first became interested in ballet I devoured books
> about dance and naively swallowed their superlatives
> about Pavlova, et al. Still omnisexual and without a
> thought of final choices (if choices they be), the fact that

I pored more over pictures of Nijinsky and [Jean] Babilée than over those of Pavlova and Karsavina would have given me a clue, had I wanted one, as to my true sexuality. Nijinsky and Babilée are comparable physical types— stocky, muscular, with a feral facial and gestural quality that comes across even in photographs. But in my fantasies Nijinsky was nonpareil. I believed all the superlatives in the books about him and Pavlova, and this belief died hard later, when I knew many who had seen them both and also many who had danced with them. Most who had merely seen them were still in thrall and only when pressed admitted that later dancers *might* be technically better. My Russian friend and short-time "husband," I.S., who knew Nijinsky and often saw him dance, assured me that his technique was sloppy and "unclassical," that when he was dancing one never saw a perfect first or fifth position, that his celebrated *ballon* was no more remarkable than many others'—but he granted him his thrilling presence. I.S. was trained at the Maryinsky school also, so I couldn't discount what he said on grounds of Moscow-Petersburg rivalry, and the two were such different physical types that they would never have been compared qua danseurs. Still, I.S. was a man and as such might be envious of Nijinsky's legendary reputation, thought I, holding on as long as possible to my fantasy of the dancing god. But even the Russian women dancers could not claim technical preeminence for him. However, I.S. and other male dancers and the females, too, were not disparaging him as an artist. What they seem to have been saying was that technique is a means to an end

(Art), and if one can reach that end with a less than perfect technique, still the end has been reached, and that Nijinsky was a man, a human being with flaws and gifts like everyone else, weaker than most perhaps, and like all, unique. . . . So my impression of Nijinsky changed from that of a superhuman to one of a frail human, in the end more to be pitied than most. Physically, I never found him particularly attractive, except for his superbly expressive neck. I much prefer, for example, Donatello's to Michelangelo's *David*, Youskevitch's lean and wiry body to Nijinsky's chunky, bulky one.

As to the question of masculine vs. feminine qualities in Nijinsky, how can we judge? The photographs suggest to me more of an ambivalence or asexuality than anything else, perhaps because of his own apparent confusion about it. One might even surmise (wildly), with his Faun in mind, that his sexual fantasies were his secret and that masturbation was his best release. But that's taking things a bit far. I would guess that his was "pure" dancing, physical of course, but unsexual, much like Eric Bruhn's, except that Bruhn had impeccable technique—one saw perfect first and fifth and even fourth positions at every turn. Perhaps I was carried away in [Francis Reeves's] description of Youskevitch's presence on stage, but when he danced he did exude a definite masculine, sexual aura—quite unlike his gentle, sweet and unassuming offstage self. The same can be said of Eglevsky, a big, beefy man with great physical ability, but who had rather effeminate mannerisms on stage, flipping up his hands, probably as a rather misguided

145

emphasis, at, say, the end of a series of pirouettes, or when he was jumping for his famous entrechats. Because of his obviously masculine and blatantly heterosexual presence, this wrist-flipping was more of an unintentional and annoying travesty than a truly effeminate gesture, and although I'm told that his penis was available at all times to any orifice, male or female, no one ever suggested that he was gay, simply that he was "oversexed" (a term, by the way, which seems to have gone out of the language). In general, although I can on occasion enjoy and indulge in effeminacy as camp and as a valid form of gay humor, I dislike it when it has become an unconscious and permanent facet of one's personality. I like males too much to be able with equanimity to see them distort what I, at least, consider the true nature of masculinity. Drag queens are, of course, a category apart, and I grant them their effeminacy with all my heart and without prejudice. But drag queens excepted, I find effeminacy as out of place on stage as in everyday life. In fact, I find *any* mannerisms out of place on stage, unless specifically called for by the role, say, of a blustering bully or a prissy, finicky old maid. Male and female bodies are in themselves sufficient statements of their sex without any underlining with extraneous gesture. (Personal communication)

M.C. has learned, along with Nijinsky, to let himself off the hook. Like Duncan Grant imitating the Specter of the Rose or Joe E. Brown reacting to Jack Lemmon's transvestism in *Some Like It Hot* (1959), he's realized that nobody's perfect. But he misunderstands the marked transvestism or "deliberate" camp he enjoys from time to time (Sontag 282). As an essentialist for whom gender is an unconscious expression of biological sex, M.C. can't quite fathom what drag queens, along with Nijinsky, have in fact been trying to tell him: that both conventional masculinity and conventional femininity are essentially performative—or theatrical.

Paris, 1912

MUSIC: HAHN

LIBRETTO: COCTEAU/MADRAZO

CHOREOGRAPHY: FOKINE

SETS AND COSTUMES: BAKST

Le Dieu bleu

*D*iaghilev wouldn't have had Nijinsky play Krishna, Hahn compose something this derivative (his India sounds like Massenet), Fokine create something this anomalous (his India looks like Siam), or Cocteau write something this silly (and derivative—his scenario recalls both *La Bayadère* [1877] and *Cléopâtre*) if the production of another Oriental number hadn't been a good idea at the time. Yet the ballet was "a failure in every sense of the word" (Valery Svetlov, *Mercure de France*, May 15, 1912). Imagine it, and in doing so ponder Susan Sontag's useful notion of "naive" camp (282).* The Blue God (Nijinsky), at the bidding of the Lotus Goddess (Lydia Nelidova), emerges from a moonlit pool to charm monsters attacking a girl (Karsavina) condemned for having prevented her lover (Max Frohman) from entering the priesthood.† He shows the Lotus Goddess what

*Critics today, regardless of Sontag's thoughts on deliberate camp, find her thoughts on naive camp—of which she cites *Swan Lake* as a random example—useless. They're more interested in strategic triviality than "failed seriousness" and more invested in gender subversion than aesthetic fiasco (Sontag 287).

†Cocteau describes the charm in static/kinetic terms: "His gestures are alternately gentle and frenetic. He leaps from one to the other with supple and terrible bounds. He glides amid their grovelling mass. Now he fascinates them with cabbalistic poses, now scares them with imperious threats. They try to drag him down, but he escapes them. At his command the tendrils of jungle plants entwine them and bind them, and the scent of blossoms overpowers them" (quoted in Hahn n.p.). Elsewhere, Cocteau says the Blue God

he's accomplished, and she gives him a flute in return. His flute solo inspires a "Dance of Divine Enchantment" and reduces the Blue God himself to a state of intoxication. Apprehensive priests cower at the sight of the miracle and free the girl on the orders of the Lotus Goddess. The lovers are reunited; he renouncing his vocation, she dancing for joy. And as the Lotus Goddess blesses the couple, the Blue God "soars to heaven on a magic golden staircase which unwinds itself beneath his feet" (Hahn n.p.).

No one found the Blue God memorable. Many found him infantile.* And few found him believable. To quote Cocteau: "At a signal from the Goddess, the Blue God left the fountain and set about charming the monsters, a task he enjoyed like a schoolboy in a circus. . . . Surely none could have felt terror at the engaging spectacle this presented! And yet the priests were frightened out of their senses" (Cocteau and Arséne, *Bakst* 19). This negative reaction, moreover, failed to plague *L'Oiseau de feu*, a popular if noncampy work in which the title character charms monsters as well. And it failed to have been modulated by Nijinsky's spectacular exit. Even though the gesture represented the last time he'd soar offstage, it wasn't worth reading that way. It was too mechanical. (Nijinsky, needing technical

-----

"vivifies for the beholder the postures of Hindu sculpture" (Ballets Russes Souvenir Program, 1912; trans. in Ries 183). Kirstein calls the posturing both brilliant and "bizarre," a word he doesn't use in relation to similar tableaux in *Danse siamoise* (*Nijinsky Dancing* 119).

*Camp, including deliberate camp, is frequently derided as infantile. Firbank's characters, for example, are often called childish.

assistance, didn't soar on his own this time.) And it didn't literalize a figure of speech. The figure "social climbing," of course, comes to mind, but the Blue God, already divine when he emerged from the pool at the beginning of the ballet, is no classier now—now that we see his transcendence yet, because he's never known abjection, fail to feel it. After all, we do demand the transcendence of abjection of—and from—art, especially if we've known abjection ourselves, as most gays have, and even when the art in issue is declassified as camp.*

Take opera. Take *Cats*. Please. At the end of that awful if somewhat campy musical (Andrew Lloyd Weber's music alone makes the show awful—an isolation move we can't perform in relation to *Le Dieu bleu*), we actually see poor Grizabella, along with Old Deuteronomy, soar atop a tire—and then, transcending abjection, climb a private stairway to paradise. It's an astonishing sight you don't forget, even if you've hated the show.

---

*The girl, of course, transcends abjection—something we don't see glorified. We do however see the analogous transcendence glorified in *La Bayadère*, one reason the ballet is more successful than *Le Dieu bleu*. Perhaps Cocteau didn't identify with Karsavina. He did identify with Nijinsky, considering him a sacred monster who, unlike the Blue God, transcended humanity by becoming an artist; an athlete who became a god by combining the grace and brutality Cocteau first noticed in *Le Spectre de la rose*; and a kindred spirit who understood the theatricalization of experience Cocteau called, not camp, but "professional deformation" (see Ries 16–17). Unfortunately, *Le Dieu bleu* conveyed none of these considerations.

Paris, 1912

MUSIC: DEBUSSY

LIBRETTO: MALLARMÉ

CHOREOGRAPHY: NIJINSKY

SETS AND COSTUMES: BAKST

❧

L'Après-midi d'un faune

(AFTERNOON OF A FAUN)

*T*he notoriety of the Parisian Faun stems from the masturbatory gesture with which Nijinsky ended his choreographic debut. Other elements of the production were innovative: the nude costume Nijinsky wore; the pedestrian quality opposed to classical ballet; the two-dimensionality opposed to theatrical convention; the movement vocabulary opposed to Debussy's music.* But the gesture alone, performed in a representational style that jibed with Nijinsky's opening solo (the Faun lying on a hill, playing a pipe, eating grapes) but jarred with the nonrepresentational style of the intervening ensembles, caused an outcry. For if no one in living memory had leapt his way on a Western stage, no one had masturbated there either. To quote Nikolai Minsky (poet, philosopher, and dance critic): "Apollo cedes place to Dionysus, and the curtain falls" (*Ultro rossii*, May 24, 1912, p. 2). To quote Gaston Calmette (editor), who imagined Nijinsky had an erection at the premiere: "We were offered an unseemly Faun who perpetrated vile, bestially erotic movements, and disgustingly shameless gestures—nothing more than that. Well-deserved hisses greeted the only-too-real-

*According to Ravel, "Debussy's symphonic poem, supple, undulating, gently tinted, and of unprecedented fluidity, stood in singular contrast to the precision, rigidity, and angular archaism of its choreographic interpretation" (404). The opposition, moreover, included the final gesture. Where "Debussy's faun opts for sustained pleasure rather than climax" (McClary 101), Nijinsky's Faun opts for climax.

istic mime, the ill-shaped animal body, and the countenance even more repellant in profile than in full face" (*Le Figaro*, May 30, 1912). Rodin, however, liked it: "Nothing could be more striking than the impulse with which, at the climax, he lies face down on the secreted veil, kissing it and hugging it to him with passionate abandon" (*Le Matin*, May 30, 1912, p. 1).* In fact, the gesture was more modest than these reports indicate— at least by today's standards. The Faun kneels on one knee, stretches out his other leg, arches his back, laughs, lowers his body onto the Nymph's veil, slides his hands down his sides, makes a barely perceptible pelvic thrust, spasms, and lies still.[†]

Modest or not, the notorious gesture, judging from reports like Calmette's and from the extent to which people who know

---

*Cocteau, mulling this over in 1953, revealed an intriguing fantasy. "After the Calmette scandal [Diaghilev] asked Rodin to make a statue of Nijinsky. . . . In the first session, when Rodin was drawing, Nijinsky was amazed to hear the sound of snoring. He was posing with his back to Rodin. He turned around. Rodin was asleep, collapsed in an armchair and his beard. The next day, the same pose—more strange noises. Nijinsky turns around. Rodin, fly open, is masturbating. The statue stopped there" (*Past Tense* 109). The story is apocryphal.

†At the premiere, Nijinsky slid his right hand under his body and made several perceptible thrusts—elements eliminated in subsequent performances but reintroduced by George de la Pena in *Nijinsky*. One post-premiere review, relying on a program book that cited Mallarmé ("A faun dozes, / Nymphs tease him, / A forgotten scarf satisfies his dream, / The centaur descends so that the poem can begin in everyone's memory"), suggests the elimination went too far. Nijinsky's "stiff poses," it notes, "and particularly his last action when he lies down to dream beside the scarf [were] extraordinarily expressive" (*The Times*, Feb. 18, 1913).

little else about Nijinsky are still aware of it, was scandalous. Now if you enter certain critical straits, you'll think that a pedestrian yet orgasmic dance like *L'Après-midi d'un faune*, being scandalous, is neither dancelike nor Dionysian. Nietzsche wrote that when man "expresses himself [sic] through song and dance as the member of a higher community, he has forgotten how to walk . . . and is on the brink of taking wing" (23). René Girard, developing this idea, writes that scandal and dance oppose one another:

> Scandal is everything that prevents us from dancing. The grace of the dancer delivers us less from our bodily infirmities, which are insignificant, than from *skandalon* itself. [*Skandalon*: a stumbling block, an obstacle that repels and attracts.] The movements of dance seem to untangle for us the otherwise unyielding knots of our desires. To enjoy the dance is to identify with the dancer; it is to dance with her [sic] and no longer to feel our imprisonment in Mallarmé's "ice" or to be mired in Sartre's "visqueux." (316)

But one needn't enter these straits or think this way, because plenty of gay men, including ones who aren't particularly enamored of Nijinsky, have in fact untangled the otherwise unyielding knots of homoerotic desire by dancing, identifying, and even having virtual sex with his pedestrian, orgasmic Faun. True, Harry Hay (founding father of the gay-rights movement and self-styled modern dance aficionado) did so by making the Faun less pedestrian than he was, removing in retrospect the scandalous obstacle of gravity. "Did I ever see Nijinsky?" Hay writes in 1995:

No, Hon, in the last Winter 1924–25 season I was still a
West Coast provincial subteen. [Think of Koestenbaum,
in San Jose, at twelve.] But as an acceptable 6′ 3″ dish, in
the Winter of 1932–33, I was whisked through LA's old
Philharmonic's orchestra pit by a lecherous older usher,
into a first row vacancy to see the great David Lichine do
L'Après-midi with similar elevations and leaps. [Nijinsky
leapt only once: a small, goatlike jump.] During the many
bows and cheers for which, I—*quite* inadvertently of
course—just happened to catch his eye . . . and was nodded
backstage. I think it was during the course of that night or,
more accurately, early the next morning, that I first heard
raptures about the fabulous Nijinsky—in beautiful broken
English.

True, Denby, writing in 1936, did so by aestheticizing and
hence de-scandalizing the Faun's orgasm:

> Most of the gestures used [do] have prototypes in Greek
> reliefs and vase paintings, but, in addition to that intellec-
> tual association with adolescence, the fact is that when
> the body imitates these poses, the kind of tension resulting
> expresses exactly the emotion Nijinsky wants to express.
> Both their actual tension and their apparent remoteness,
> both their plastic clarity and their emphasis by negation
> on the center of the body (it is always strained between
> the feet in profile and the shoulders en face)—all these
> qualities lead up to the complete realization of the Faun's
> last gesture. The poignancy of this moment lies partly in
> the complete change in the direction of tension, in the

satisfying relief that results; and the substitution of a new tension (the incredible backbend) gives the work its balance. But besides, the eye has been educated to see the plastic beauty of this last pose, and the rhythmic sense to appreciate its noble deliberateness. That it is so intensely human a gesture, coming after a long preparation of under-statement, gives it, in its cumulative assurance, the force of an illumination. ("Nijinsky's 'Faun'" 39)

But Rorem (self-styled narcissist and neoromantic composer) untangled those knots shortly thereafter (in 1937), regardless of the Nietzschean imperative. He performed, that is, his scan-dalous, pre-orgasmic "Dance of the Adolescents"—for him, as for Hay, it was a duet with a boyfriend, not a solo—without imagining even in retrospect that Lichine took wing, yet with-out feeling imprisoned in Mallarmé's ice.

At home in our living room Perry [O'Neil] and I (blush!) re-created *L'Après-midi d'un faune,* using a mess of incense, scarves from Mother's cedar chest, and the tastelessly tasteful Stokowski record which gave new meaning to the concept of rubato by stretching solo lines of flute and oboe into an irresistable excruciation of silver taffy. Ah well, as the ever-wise Montaigne decreed: "It needs at least as much perfection to develop an empty theme as to sustain a weighty one." So Perry and I, like every adolescent in history (except maybe Rimbaud), confusing enthusiasm with self-expression, and self-expression with art, developed to perfection our empty theme.

To this spectacle—so oft rehearsed, so amateur—we invited the Osatos [a couple whose daughter Sono was a member of the Ballets Russes]. Frances [Osato] came with her younger Nisei daughter Teru, who, after my sister, Rosemary, was the most beautiful girl I'd ever seen, all ivory and jet and peach, with a smile inscrutably American. For them we danced our duet. Perry, I'm afraid, played the nymph, short hair and hirsute thighs, whisking out of sight at crucial moments to turn over the Red Seal disc. I "danced" the faun, inviolable and icy, ruminating on David Lichine's slow-motion antics, while audibly sniffling mucus as I sounded an invisible reed. (97)

Pre-orgasmic? Sustained pleasure rather than blissful climax? Rorem himself explains:

Perry, meanwhile, and I understandably went "all the way" with our sentimental revels. Not just *The Afternoon of a Faun*, but *Daphnis and Chloë*, *The Rite of Spring*, and tens of other Stokowski interpretations whose sensuous exaggeration goaded us down the primrose path. We "had sex," lost our cherries—if that loss can be defined through non-ejaculatory friction. . . . Ejaculatory friction came months later with D., more male than Perry, with gnarled biceps and ruddy cheeks. D. had gained cachet on the block not only by being a super athlete with super grades, and by playing the risky game of pressing our neck arteries so as to produce in us a popperlike swoon, but [by] teaching other boys to cum. When in the intimacy of his gray sheets he brought me to orgasm I thought something terribly wrong had exploded in my urethra. Yet for a week I masturbated three times a day, winnowing that down to twice, then once a day for months. (98–99)

Narcissistic? Nijinsky's Faun, unlike his Narcissus, is free of death-driven vanity if not carnality.* His masturbatory gesture is supposed to involve the Nymph, the Other—or her veil, in a metonymic and fetishistic substitution.† And Rorem's "Dance of the Adolescents" was a pas de deux. Once again, Rorem himself explains:

> Earlier in these pages I hinted that as a child I felt the cosmos to be my own invention, and that I still to some extent believe this. I did not magnanimously add, Don't we all?, because the "we" was also, by definition, my fabrication. Do I then feel alone in the universe? Yes, except that the universe does not exist except in my conditioned imagination. (Conditioned by whom?) Life is merely one minor possible result of the Big Bang. Reality's dreary, art's

---

*See Burt: the final gesture is "a deliberate provocation to society to condemn such spontaneous sexual behavior, as if he were saying that only a depraved mind could see anything depraved in this" (92).

†Cf. Garafola: "The scarf that he hugs to himself [is not] merely a stand-in for its absent owner. Equally, it symbolizes his triumph over the snares of Woman, his resistance to the temptation of her flesh. In [*L'Après-midi d'un faune*], where Nijinsky the overt homosexual declared himself a covert heterosexual, the fetishism of the scarf bespoke a deep-rooted ambivalence toward men and women alike. Torn between the power of his lust and the fear of its consequences, Nijinsky opted for the safe haven of self-gratification" (*Diaghilev* 57).

dreary. Those quadrillion lifeless galaxies out there are surely as curious, as *potential*, as Earth, which we perceive with only our five miserable senses. Yet I alone created and imagine it. Did I too create my own limited perceptions, an inability to grasp the nuances of philosophy, government systems, mathematical formulas? Did I create them so as *not* to understand them?

Maybe that's all guff, but it's me, my paragraph. Still the paragraph can't explain, since I myself can't, a lingering remoteness from other people and their concerns. It *does* explain my ease at aping Mallarmé's faun, French par excellence. But if France means cool, or at least objective, why can I, who am distant, be so moved by that country's art, while finding the universe—be it God's or mine—so second rate? (100–101)

This indicates troublesome slippages from masturbation to narcissism and from narcissism to solipsism—troublesome insofar as they imply a lack of political interest in Others who don't happen to be gay as well ("a lingering remoteness from other people and their concerns"). That's the problem with making something of Nijinsky's Faun. The character moves across a range of gay stereotypes—adolescent, masturbatory, narcissistic, fetishistic, superficial (two-dimensional), scandalous—leaving us to transvalue them, which is easy, and to eradicate their negative connotations, which isn't. Try it some time. Nijinsky, literally soaring, may have reconfigured gay male flight; you, however, can't flaunt your stereotypical sexuality in a manner everyone finds agreeable. You transvalue gay adolescence, thinking "I'm so youthful." Others, scandalized, are thinking, "He's so retarded." You transvalue gay superficiality, thinking "I'm so stylish." Others are thinking, "He's so glib." But we have no other choice. We can't be gay nor can we be queer without negotiating such stereotypes to the best of our abilities, even if like Rorem's Faun—or the Faun Rorem, using meaningful quotation marks, says he "danced"—these negotiations are inept.*

Consider Van Vechten's impression of Nijinsky's Faun. In "Secret of the Russian Ballet," he mentions, in passing, the little leap.

> [The leaps in *Jeux*] are triumphs of dexterity, grace of motion, and thrill, and he does not waste them. They have given rise to the rumor that Nijinsky's element is the air. In *L'Après-midi d'un faune* he makes only one of these quick movements, but with such astonishing effect that on one occasion (it was the third time I had seen this stage arrangement of Debussy's prelude to Mallarmé's poem) my companion, a well-known dramatic critic who sits stolidly through performances by all the great tragedians, burst into tears. (77)

In the essay "The Russian Ballet and Nijinsky," however, Van Vechten dwells on the Faun's adolescent glee (*jouissance*) and not on his own sadness (*tristesse*). "A thing of beauty is a boy forever," he writes in an epigraph attributed to Allen Norton and reminiscent of Keats's *Endymion*. It's no joke, or isn't sim-

---

*"Fags" remain "fags" even after the aborted French revolution of 1968, according to Guy Hocquenghem in *L'Après-Mai des faunes*.

ply a joke in Van Vechten's fiction, which takes the stereotype "gay adolescence" seriously—transvaluing and transfiguring it as much as was possible at the time. The line "A thing of beauty is a boy forever" reappears in *The Blind Bow-Boy* (1923) as the motto of homosexual Ronald Middlebottom, a Firbankian figure.* The garden of Middlebottom's Manhattan home features "a fountain inspired by Nijinsky's interpretation of Mallarmé's faun" (124)—as opposed to the fountain of cupid "about to discharge an arrow at random" (158–59) in the garden of Campaspe Lorillard, a woman who, according to Middlebottom, resembles the Firebird (Karsavina). In other words, one negative connotation of "gay adolescence"—indiscriminate promiscuity—is displaced within the purview of a nongay and nonmale character. Van Vechten even associates a second heterosexual female (Zimbule O'Grady) with both the negative connotation and the Faun: "she is an animal, and she will only be happy so long as she lives like an animal, naturally and a little libidinously" (156).

In *Peter Whiffle* (1922), which reiterates "A thing of beauty is a boy forever," Van Vechten tries to turn "gay adolescence" away from its stereotypical connotation of unadulterated *jouissance*, returning to it—or turning it into—some of his companion's tristesse. At twenty-one, "gay, faun-like" Peter Whiffle took "the keenest joy in everything he did" (180, 199)—joy, moreover, Van Vechten associates with Nijinsky. Donatello's *David*, Whiffle remarks, "is the most beautiful statue I have

---

*Middlebottom is "a silver flamingo . . . glowing, glamorous, shining—like Galahad in armour—and strange, aloof; he [does] not mate with the rose flamingos" (131–32).

ever seen, just as Debussy's *L'Après-midi d'un faune* is the most beautiful music I have ever heard" (203). And Whiffle himself looks like Nijinsky: "Peter [now thirty-four] was the first to undress and, as he stood on the parapet of the pool by the broken column, his body glowing rose-ivory in the soft light of the setting sun, his head a mass of short black curls, he seemed a part of the scene, a strange visitor from the old faun-like epoch, and I could imagine a faint playing of pipes beyond the wall, and a row of Tanagra nymphs fleeing, terrified, in basso-rilievo" (198). But Whiffle dies young, shortly after that sunset, casting his adolescent *jouissance* in a different light. "As I write these lines," Van Vechten sighs, "I could fancy that he stands beside me, a sombrely joyous spectre" (197). This tristesse is embedded in Whiffle's premature death (another gay stereotype), Debussy's music (most beautiful, but sad as well), and the scandalous orgasm that haunts the sombrely joyous specter of Nijinsky's Faun.* It's also embedded in a gay stereotype as negative, for those of us no longer in our first youth (I, at thirty-six, am now there), as tragic early death: the stereotype of the sad old queen. Sad because we're supposed to be lonely. Think of Aschenbach at the end of his life. Think, for that matter, of Van Vechten, Hay, or even Rorem at the end of theirs—because, despite the stereotype, none of them did, or are now doing, too badly! Rorem, of course, enjoys the advantage of youthful good looks. But the others don't. Nor do I, who am neither sad nor lonely—or no sadder and

---

*Male orgasm, figuratively speaking, is a little death (*petit mort*) if not a love-death (*Liebestod*) and a prelude, mythically speaking, to post-coital—and post-masturbatory—despair.

no lonelier than the next heterosexual guy, which may be what some find scandalous about me. I'm atypical. I don't fit the mold. My *jouissance* isn't, or is no longer, tinged with sadness—returning me to, or turning me into, the stereotype of the adolescent with an erection, which would be scandalous as well if like Nijinsky I ever masturbated in public.

Langston Hughes, not long after the publication of *Peter Whiffle* and *The Blind Bow-Boy*, wrote "Nude Young Dancer" (1925), a poem about both Josephine Baker and Nijinsky.

What jungle tree have you slept under
Midnight dancer of the jazzy hour?
What great forest has hung its perfume
Like a sweet veil about your bower?

What jungle tree have you slept under,
Dark brown girl of the swaying hips?
What stark-white moon has been your lover?
To what mad faun have you offered your lips?

(Reprinted in Watkins 168)

We know Hughes means Nijinsky because the faun is mad. We know he means Nijinsky's Faun because of the dancer's nudity and because of the metaphoric veil about his or her bower.* We even know he may have had Van Vechten's Nijinsky in mind

---

*Garafola uses another metaphoric veil to make an important point about the Faun: "In dispensing with exoticism, the convention that made the portrayal of lust in *Schéhérazade* [and] *Cléopâtre* at once exciting and morally innocuous, Nijinsky stripped the veil of ritualized fantasy from the representation of sexuality" (*Diaghilev* 308). Baker, however, dispensed with neither exoticism nor primitivism.

because of the reference to Endymion ("What stark-white moon has been your lover?"). What's interesting if not depressing about this poem is that Hughes, skirting scandal, turns an attractive male dancer into an attractive female, a displacement for which compulsory heterosexuality if not homophobia is to blame; turns an autoerotic orgasm into a heteroerotic kiss, a displacement for which an aversion to masturbation and narcissism if not solipsism is to blame; and, following through on Baker's gender, turns the Faun into the Nymph—moving from "What stark-white moon has been your lover?" to "To what mad faun have you offered you lips?"

Notice I don't blame Hughes's transformation of the orgasm into the kiss on an aversion to Dionysian dance. Any attraction to Baker, even one that masks an attraction to Nijinsky, is an attraction to manic exuberance. Think of her "Banana" Dance. Hughes, in other words, is no George Balanchine, who in *Apollo* (1928) restrains Nijinsky's feral bliss.* Nor is Hughes José Limón, who in *The Moor's Pavane* (1949) sets the Nymph's veil, the Faun's backbend, and the Faun's masturbatory gesture in a heterosexual context with a blatant gay subtext.† Nor is he

---

*Lifar, who danced the Faun five days before he first danced Apollo, enacted this restraint. See Scholl: "Balanchine's Apollo begins where Nijinsky's Faun left off: the supremely dionysian act that concluded Nijinsky's work is a point of departure for Balanchine, whose choreography conveys in one terse gesture the 'wild, half-human' quality of the youth who will acquire 'nobility through art'" (79). Autoeroticism, moreover, has no place in *Apollo*. Neither, in the final analysis, does two-dimensionality.

†When the Moor's Friend (Iago) taunts the Moor (Othello) by getting down on his knees, arching his back, and rubbing the handkerchief of the Moor's Wife (Desdemona) against his own body from his crotch to his face, "Iago is

Jerome Robbins, who in *Afternoon of a Faun* (1953) skirts Nijinsky's scandal by turning the autoerotic orgasm into a heteroerotic kiss by a narcissistic danseur on a ballerina's cheek—an even fainter echo of the sexual implications (hetero as well as homo) of Nijinsky's final gesture. At least Hughes's dancer has herself kissed on the lips.

Two of the Faun's queer dance incarnations, however, have restored the scandalous, Dionysian aspects of the final gesture and improved on Van Vechten's partial eradication of its stereotypicality. In *La Faune* (1987), Marie Chouinard uses a blushing phallus to make her solo's final moment as startling as Nijinsky's.* Ann Cooper Albright, a postmodern critic, describes how:

> Working always in profile, Chouinard uses only a thin downstage slice of the space, traversing the stage laterally, back and forth, back and forth. She is dressed in a skin-colored unitard with extra padding on one thigh and the other calf, and a headpiece consisting of two large ramlike horns. Still, poised with the attentiveness of a hunter, her gaze steadily scans the horizon as a soundtrack of repetitive breathing gradually crescendos. Her steps are bulky and uneven, belying a fiercely bound sexual energy which

---

implying that he has had sex with Desdemona and thus that Othello is a cuckold . . . but the manner in which Iago conveys this draws Othello's attention to the sexual attraction of Iago's own body" (Burt 126–27).

*Chouinard isn't the first female dancer to attempt the Faun. Nijinska, with whom Nijinsky created the role, as well as the role of the Chosen One in *Le Sacre du printemps*, performed it—straight—in 1922.

explodes unexpectedly in thrusts and quivers of her pelvis. Time and again a contraction grips her body, bringing her to her knees. As the breathing becomes louder and louder, it takes on an industrial, almost menacing quality. What was once an internal accompaniment to Chouinard's movements becomes an external, oppressive sound, forcing her to continue. Images of an injured animal, a predator, a bacchant, even of Nijinsky himself dart across this tableau. Then Chouinard breaks off a section of her horn and attaches it to her crotch. What previously had been an image, a movement quality, crystallizes into a surreal moment as Chouinard, exausted after an increasingly forceful series of pelvic thrusts, moves into Nijinsky's final pose. (175)

Surreal—or all too real, like the original ending. Someone—or something—other than the Nymph, however, provokes the pelvic thrusts of this androgynous creature. Chouinard replaces the objects of Nijinsky's desire (the Nymph, her veil) with rays of light because she finds "the ambivalence of the object of desire . . . marvelous" (quoted in Albright 175)—even, or perhaps especially, when that object is the Faun(e) him-or-herself, a possibility Albright refuses to call narcissistic:

In addition to physicalizing the faun's desire, she also occupies the spotlight of that which is desired: the nymph, the scarf, the woman, the "other." Shifting in and out of this intangible light, Chouinard "steps" back and forth between . . . faun and nymph, Nijinsky and herself. . . . As in the writing of [Jacques] Derrida . . . Chouinard's performance of *La Faune* crosses over these boundaries of "self" and "other" so frequently that the very categories begin to lose their meaning. (177)

But perhaps Albright, like *La Faune*'s phallus, is a bit too sanguine. Even postmodern audience members might be reminded once again of premature—and stereotypical—gay death. Chouinard's costume, unlike Nijinsky's, has dartlike projections attached to it. According to Albright "it is ambiguous whether they symbolize horns of the faun, the literal expression of the faun's sexuality, or the arrows of a hunter" (177). Or whether they symbolize the arrows of St. Sebastian, that transcendental—and sentimental—signifier of premature gay death.

Rubinstein, as mentioned in connection with *Le Spectre de la rose*, had played the saint in the 1911 premiere of D'Annunzio's *Le Martyre de St. Sébastien*—a production that scandalized Frenchmen who claimed it was sacrilegious for a Jewish woman to represent a Christian martyr. The reactions to both Rubinstein's premiere and Nijinsky's one year later anticipated the reaction to the Faun's second queer incarnation. When Mark Morris masturbated to orgasm as the Sorceress in the Brussels premiere of *Dido and Aeneas* (1989) even he sensed the shock of the scandalized Belgians who, because they'd never seen a woman, let alone a man dressed as a woman, do such a thing on a legitimate stage, didn't know how to describe what they saw stereotypically. (Belgium, like France, is predominantly Catholic and deeply conservative.) They were simply—and blissfully—at a loss for conventionally derogatory words.

Paris, 1912

MUSIC: RAVEL

LIBRETTO: LONGUS/FOKINE

CHOREOGRAPHY: FOKINE

SETS AND COSTUMES: BAKST

✤

Daphnis et Chloé

I'd love to have seen or to read an account of the *Daphnis et Chloé* Rorem and O'Neil performed on their way to going all the way with one another and, assuming Rorem played Daphnis (Nijinsky), wonder whether O'Neil played Darkon (Bolm), the rival for Chloë's affection. I'd like to think he did, even though he was the Nymph in their *L'Après-midi d'un faune* and even though it makes sense for O'Neil, Rorem's first boyfriend, to have been Chloë (Karsavina), Daphnis's first girlfriend. For, in addition to being lovers, Rorem and O'Neil were competitors. They were the two best musicians in their high school and as such vied with one another for the title of single best. At the time, Rorem resented that O'Neil was the better pianist, which may have led him to assign O'Neil the role of inferior dancer (Bolm) and vanquished rival (Darkon). Over time, Rorem came to realize that he was the better composer—and that O'Neil was a failed virtuoso, a turnabout he still savors.* Nor are

* "Perry, after premiering Ravel's *Left-hand Concerto* rippingly with the WPA's new Illinois Symphony under Madame Antonia Brico in 1941, premiering my own Second Sonata on WQXR in its first version ten years later, and recording the four MacDowell sonatas on a small label, suddenly quit. He was a terrific pianist, far better than I, with an infallible metronomic instinct, mercurial fingers in Rachmaninoff as in Scarlatti, a neat, ruby tone, and a dependable, caring style in chamber music. But as [a] prodigy confronting the real world he found the rat race unremunerative, threw in the sponge, and become a librarian. Today he lives quietly on Jane Street with his friend Tom and never listens to Stokowski" (Rorem 99).

Rorem and O'Neil the only gay men or the only musicians to find themselves caught up in homoerotic—as opposed to homosocial—competition. Chopin and Liszt found themselves so, as did Vladimir Horowitz and Arthur Rubinstein. (Chopin was the better composer, Liszt the better pianist; Horowitz the more popular pianist, Rubinstein the classier one.) Gay men, in other words, are basically men. We're trained to see life as a zero-sum game (you win, I lose) and likely to agonize our love lives by having them rehearse primordial conflicts—filial, fraternal, mythic. Far too many of us wonder who's smarter, sexier, stronger, healthier, saner, better educated, better looking, better developed, better immunized, better analyzed—a situation that we may never outgrow and that still requires both aesthetic and erotic expression.

Daphnis et Chloé, for Rorem and O'Neil, must have done the trick on several levels. On an orchestral level, it recapitulated a rivalry between Debussy, a heterosexual composer, and Ravel, a homosexual one, that the young American musicians were interested in. Debussy and Ravel, in general, vied with one another for the title of leading impressionist, Ravel following in Debussy's footsteps yet surpassing his popularity. *Daphnis et Chloé* is an exception. Even though it matches the supple, undulating, gently tinted, and unprecedented fluidity of *Prélude à l'Après-midi d'un faune* note for note, Debussy's masterpiece is more familiar to modern listeners. On a choreographic level, it incorporated the rivalry between Fokine, a heterosexual dancer, and Nijinsky, a bisexual one. To Nijinsky's credit, this rivalry was rather unilateral. Fokine alone, who up until *L'Après-midi d'un faune* had choreographed every Ballets

Russes production, resented having to share the spotlight with an inexperienced upstart and hated having been upstaged by him.* Nijinsky's mind simply didn't work that way, which made him seem queerer than he, in fact, was.

Daphnis et Chloé must have done the trick on narratological and mythic levels as well. In the ballet, Chloë inadvertently attracts Darkon, a cowherd who tries to kiss her. Daphnis pushes Darkon away and the villagers propose a dance contest between the two, the prize to be a kiss from Chloë. (Their rivalry is homosocial, not homoerotic.) Drums and bassoons introduce Darkon's dance, one with more archaic and angular movements than those of the others. His grotesque performance, punctuated by trombone glissandi, is ridiculed by the spectators, who burst out laughing (staccato woodwind chords). Now Daphnis dances, his arms around a staff that rests on his shoulders (slow flutes, with harp glissandi to allow for Nijinsky's leaps). Daphnis, victorious, kisses Chloë (oboe solo) and has Darkon chased away. Daphnis, here, is both Marsyas and Apollo, flute and harp, making him lucky not to have been flayed alive.

In nonnarrative theater dance, male competition has less dire consequences. Tap dancers, for example, applaud one another even as they best one another. So do break dancers. Unfortunately, classical ballet is both narrative and hierarchical. It's a system in which only stars with certain skills and physiques play leading roles. Fokine, for all his innovations, endorsed this

Daphnis et Chloé was a commercial failure; *L'Après-midi d'un faune,* despite—or because of—the scandal, was a success.

177

system, awarding the Specter of the Rose to Nijinsky and the Firebird to Karsavina because they soared above the company they helped keep. But neither love nor sex, whether heterosexual or homosexual, is necessarily narrative. If narrative, they aren't necessarily competitive. And if competitive, they aren't necessarily agonistic. Lovers, like tap and break dancers, can compete in order to elicit one another's best if nonidentical efforts. Instead of you win, I lose—you win, I win. Instead of anything you can do, I can do better—you do this well, I do that well. Or, we both do this well. Love, in other words, is a theater in which no one should be seen as grotesque or made to feel like a failure. Even Darkon—even O'Neil—doesn't deserve his erotic fate.

Paris, 1913

MUSIC: DEBUSSY

LIBRETTO: DIAGHILEV/BAKST/NIJINSKY

CHOREOGRAPHY: NIJINSKY

SETS AND COSTUMES: BAKST

✤

Jeux

*F*or Nijinsky, *Jeux* depicted Diaghilev sandwiched between Nijinsky himself and another lover. The ballet, he wrote in his diary, "is about three young men making love to each other."

> The *Faun* is me, and *Jeux* is the life of which Diaghilev dreamed. He wanted to have two boys as lovers. He often told me so, but I refused. Diaghilev wanted to make love to two boys at the same time, and wanted these boys to make love to him. In the ballet, the two girls [Karsavina and Ludmilla Schollar] represent the two boys and the young man [Nijinsky] is Diaghilev. I changed the characters, as love between three men could not be represented on the stage. (140–41)

It also depicted, for Nijinsky, Duncan Grant playing tennis in Bedford Square at twilight—an inspirational match that entered the myth of Bloomsbury. To quote a poem by William Plomer that ends with a line for which both Nijinsky and Bakst have been credited:

> Nijinsky, seeing the ballet
> of tennis players in white
> darting between the tall, theatrical
> and sepia-mottled columns of the vaulting trees,
> threw out a dancer's arm, and called
> in a faun's warm voice
> "Ah, quel décor!"
> (Excerpted in Turnbaugh, *Duncan Grant* 47)

Given the minimal plot of *Jeux* and the dynamics of Grant's bisexual history, as opposed to Diaghilev's homosexual one, the latter depiction seems more apt.* Like *L'Après-midi d'un faune*, *Jeux* involves seduction fantasies. Unlike it, the dancers—tennis players—flirt, embrace, couple, regroup, pose, observe, and caress themselves. To quote Garafola, "with its ephemeral matings, voyeuristic foreplay, and obsessive self-involvement, the ballet is about the pervasiveness of desire and the avoidance of sexual entanglement" ("Nijinsky" 15). True enough, of Grant if not Diaghilev or Nijinsky. Unfortunately, Garafola, comparing the final moments of the two ballets, reduces Nijinsky (but not Diaghilev) to a queer combination of homosexual and heterosexual stereotypes—the narcissist (homosexual stereotype) wary of real women (heterosexual stereotype):

Throughout the ballet, detachment follows attachment, each brief encounter giving rise to its solipsistic opposite. Again and again, the action comes back to the desirous, desiring self who stands apart, watching the others couple, while gesturing to one or another of the body's erotic loci—breast, waist, crotch, neck. Even when the pairs—mixed or same sex—and the threesome embrace, the gaze of the individuals is averted, as if sex were not only divorced from feeling, but from awareness of another human presence, as

*The plot is akin to that of *Les Sylphides*. Each ballet contains one man and several women within "a narrative which neither suggests nor precludes concrete relationships among the principal dancers" (Scholl 95).

if, under any guise, it were merely a form of self-gratifica-tion. In *Faune*, of course, the final gesture had conveyed this with notorious directness. But where the women there were essentially projections of the Faun's erotic fantasies, in *Jeux* they are mirror images of the protagonist's com-pound sexual identity. One can go further: if his diffidence dresses masculinity in the garb of femaleness, their vigor dresses femininity in the garb of malehood. But these women are "men" of a special kind: their same-sex dal-liance marks them as Sapphic or "third-sex" males. Their flirtation intrigues the Young Man. . . . At the same time, it arouses his jealousy, and in the one decisive action he takes in the ballet, he puts an end to it. If, before, he had hesitated between the two masculinized women, now, in their guise as feminized men, he chooses them both. But this solution induces even greater anxiety, and as in *Faune*, when the moment of consummation approaches, Nijinsky employs an object to prevent nature from taking its course. In this case, his deus ex machina is a wayward ball. Fright-ening the Young Man's playmates, it salvages desire by resurrecting a surrogate object—solitary fantasy. *Jeux*, the second installment of Nijinsky's erotic autobiography, reveals, no less urgently than *Faune*, the power of desire, the ambiguity of sexual identity, and his aversion to inter-course itself. (*Diaghilev* 62–63)

In *Jeux*'s original scenario it's a wayward airplane, not a way-ward ball, that terminates the game by crashing into the tennis court—an ending less easy to stage, an object as easy to fetishize, and an image easier to associate with modernity if not sexuality.*

For Grant, who depicted Nijinsky playing tennis both before and after Nijinsky depicted him, the dancer—now Westernized—was an inspiration as well. In 1912, exploiting the game's association with both modernity and (sublimated) sexuality, inverting in advance Nijinsky's male-to-female ratio, emphasizing athleticism, and working with a lover (Adrian Stephen, Virginia Woolf's youngest brother), Grant painted a mural of one female and two male tennis players—both men nude, both Nijinsky—in the sitting room of the home he shared with John Maynard Keynes, another lover. The room overlooks the tennis court in Brunswick Square. And the movement style of the mural, if a static art form can be said to have a movement style, is dancelike. Not, however, like the dance of *Jeux*, derived from eurythmics, but like the dance of Matisse.† In 1913, however, after *Jeux*'s London premiere, Grant did design a figure of a young man wearing tennis clothes and striking a pose typical of the "cubist"—or eurythmic—ballet.

*The airplane idea was jettisoned along with that of having the three dance *en pointe*. If they had done so, *Jeux* might have been popular and it's gender interplay more pronounced. As Diaghilev informed Debussy: "lots of *pointe* for all THREE. Great secret—because up till the present *never* have men danced on toe. He would be the *first* to do so" (quoted in Garafola, "Nijinsky" 11).

†Marie Rambert, a student of Emile Jaques-Dalcroze, helped Nijinsky choreograph both *Jeux* and *Le Sacre du printemps*. Duncan Grant, Roger Fry, and Vanessa Bell (Woolf's sister) were the first Britons to appreciate a number of French modernists, including Matisse.

Bloomsbury did this sort of thing all the time. Its members were fascinated by themselves, by one another, and by aliens who entered their orbit—and rarely hesitated to show it. Woolf, confusing art and life, published *Orlando* (1928), a love letter to Vita Sackville-West. Grant created a domestic environment for one lover with the help of another and by using an artistic yet athletic figure to whom all three were devoted. In other words, he stationed Nijinsky where anyone could see him, making beautiful yet muscular gestures he admired. *Quel décor*, indeed. Not that the mural was pornographic. Sports figures, including tennis players, indicate physical prowess more readily than sublimated sexuality, which explains why Grant painted it in the sitting room and not the bedroom.* But perhaps he would have painted it in the bedroom if he'd already seen Nijinsky play tennis in *Jeux*, an aesthetic desublimation of the sport's sexuality. Or so I'm led to believe by Denby who, looking at a photograph, wrote: "I am also very moved by the uplifted, half-unclenched hands in the *Jeux* picture, as mysterious as breathing in sleep" ("Notes" 19).

*Twyla Tharp, using boxers, and Mark Morris, using wrestlers, capitalize on this disparity.

Paris, 1913

MUSIC: STRAVINSKY

LIBRETTO: STRAVINSKY/ROERICH

CHOREOGRAPHY: NIJINSKY

SETS AND COSTUMES: ROERICH

Le Sacre du printemps

(THE RITE OF SPRING)

*L*e Sacre du printemps, as anyone familiar with modernism can recall, caused a riot. Many who attended the premiere found the score, the decor, and the dance itself both ugly and tedious. Lytton Strachey, for example, hadn't "imagined that boredom and sheer anguish could have been combined together at such a pitch" (quoted in Holroyd 2: 95). Others didn't find them so, or pretended not to. Ravel, for one, enjoyed the ballet. But the naysayers were in the majority—aesthetes or philistines who failed to understand Stravinsky's irregular rhythm, appreciate Roerich's Native American design, and applaud Nijinsky's bizarre movement style. For whereas *Jeux* and *L'Après-midi d'un faune* were somewhat graceful, *Le Sacre du printemps* was thoroughly unballetic. Percussive dancers faced one another, ignoring the audience, and then stomped, lurched, and trembled their way into expressionism and oblivion.* One dancer in particular: the Chosen One (Maria Piltz), a grotesque and hysterical Giselle who danced herself to death for the good of a community too primeval—or preromantic— to know heartbreak.†

*Levinson, analogizing Josephine Baker to the Chosen One, claimed that whereas ballet follows musical phraseology in series of tensions and relaxations, primitive dance, whether "savage" or folk, is essentially rhythmic. See Watkins 140–44.

†The Chosen One performed her solo center stage and facing the audience—the ballet's only exception to its exclusion of the audience.

Some would have Nijinsky perform the solo, a grotesque and hysterical Albrecht no Giselle can save. Nijinska, who worked with Nijinsky on the role, recalled the Chosen One's death as Nijinsky's. Marie Rambert, a coworker who saw him demonstrate the role, recalled a ferocity Piltz couldn't even approximate. Garafola picks up Nijinska's thread: "Like the Golden Slave in *Schéhérazade*, the Chosen Virgin expires in an ecstasy of self-immolation; like Petrouchka, she takes upon herself the sins of the artist, the wages of psychic difference" (*Diaghilev* 71). Buckle picked up Rambert's:

> One afternoon Nijinsky rehearsed with [Piltz] alone, only Rambert being present. The latter watched in silent dismay, for Piltz could not see what was needed. Nijinsky showed her the dance. If only *he* could have taken the role, thought Rambert, if only the Harvest God could have been propitiated with a male sacrifice, this might have been Nijinsky's most wonderful creation. With clenched hand across his face, he threw himself into the air in paroxysms of fear and grief. His movements were stylized and controlled, yet he gave out a tremendous power of tragedy. It was a unique rendering of the solo by its creator, something to be remembered for ever. (283)

So did Kirstein, who felt the solo required "the sinews of a male" (*Nijinsky Dancing* 145).

Other gays have had "Nijinsky" actually perform it. Glen Tetley once danced both Nijinsky and his female victim—compounding, for some, the bad taste of the original solo and the bad taste of marked female impersonation. And Frank Bidart, in "The War of Vaslav Nijinsky" (1983), imagines what Nijinsky himself—death-driven, guilt-ridden, and nearly mad—might have meant by that performance.

—The second part of my ballet
Le Sacre du Printemps

is called "THE SACRIFICE."

A young girl, a virgin, is chosen
to die
so that the Spring will return,—

so that her Tribe (free
from "*pity*," "*introspection*," "*remorse*")

out of her blood
can renew itself.

The fact that the earth's renewal
requires human blood

is unquestioned; a mystery.

She is chosen, from the whirling, stamping
circle of her peers, purely by chance—;

then, driven from the circle, surrounded
by the elders, by her peers, by animal
skulls impaled on pikes,

she dances,—

at first, in paroxysms
of Grief, and Fear:—

again and again, she leaps (—*NOT*

as a ballerina leaps, as if she
loved the air, as if
the air were her element—)

SHE LEAPS

BECAUSE SHE HATES THE GROUND.

But then, slowly, as others
join in, she finds that there is a self

WITHIN herself

that is *NOT* HERSELF

impelling her to accept,—and at last
to *LEAD*,—

THE DANCE

that is her own sacrifice. . .

—In the end, exhausted, she falls
to the ground. . .

She dies; and her last breath
is the reawakened Earth's

orgasm,—

a little upward run on the flutes
mimicking

(—or perhaps MOCKING—)

the god's spilling
seed. . .

The Chosen Virgin
accepts her fate: without considering it,

she knows that her Tribe,—
the Earth itself,—

                    are UNREMORSEFUL

that the price of continuance
is her BLOOD:—

                    she *accepts* their guilt,—
. . . *THEIR GUILT*

THAT THEY DO NOT KNOW EXISTS.

She has become, to use
our term,
            a *Saint.*

The dancer I chose for this role
detested it.

She would have preferred to do
a fandango, with a rose in her teeth. . .

The training she and I shared,—

training in the traditional
                    "academic" dance,—

emphasizes the illusion
                    of *Effortlessness,*
Ease, Smoothness, Equilibrium. . .

When I look into my life,

these are not the qualities

I find there. (33–35)*

For men like Kirstein, Tetley, and Bidart, assuming they still embrace the romantic ideology of the feminine scapegoat (Giselle), the perfect—and perfectly beautiful—Chosen One might be an unmarked female impersonator: Nijinsky, that is, but Nijinsky passing as either Piltz or Nijinska.† Men like Strachey, however, even if they don't embrace the postromantic ideology of the masculine scapegoat (the Golden Slave), find such beauty unappealing. Whether averse to aestheticism, modernism, or simply boredom, they might prefer a perfectly—and

---

*Some, of course, wouldn't have Nijinsky perform the solo. Fans of *The Red Shoes*, a transparent if not transvestite heterosexualization of the Diaghilev affair, are content to see Moira Shearer, as Nijinsky, dance herself to death at the behest of Massine in a ballet too romantic—and pretty—to be *Le Sacre du printemps*. (The film, in fact, aligns the ballet with *Giselle*.) And every dancer other than Tetley to attempt the Chosen One in *Le Sacre du printemps* itself has been female.

†See Scholl: by doing away "with the old ballet's chief protagonist—the village maiden—while the village watches," *Le Sacre du printemps* "deals the death blow to the nineteenth-century academic ballet" (73, 77). Cf. Garafola: "At the heart of the ballet's synthetic myth is the *fin-de-siècle* obsession with the 'feminized' artist, that enervated androgyne of symbolist fiction, painting, and drama. In *Sacre*, however, the image has been tamed; shorn of its subversive sexuality, it assumes the 'safe' guise of a young girl, ballet's traditional instrument of redemption. A Giselle reimagined through the primitivism of the golden horde, the Chosen Virgin is, above all, a creation of twentieth-century male sexual anxiety" ("Nijinsky" 26).

194

deliberately—ugly Chosen One. Their Chosen One might be like Tetley a marked but unlike Tetley a campy female impersonator: "Divine," that is, but Divine failing to pass as Nijinsky. Which happens to be one of the grotesque and hysterical features of *Female Trouble*, the film Divine made with John Waters in 1974, the year Tetley tried to be Nijinsky as well.

In *Female Trouble*, Divine plays Dawn Davenport, a "model" who in two stunning solos dances herself—and others—into early graves.* Dawn performs the first solo in a go-go bar. She performs the second in a nightclub, shortly after strangling her daughter Taffy (Mink Stole), another Chosen One, in the middle of the girl's "Hare Krishna" dance. Dawn hadn't wanted Taffy to join the cult. Divine, at Waters's instance, was used to dealing with adversaries in this manner. In *Eat Your Makeup* (1968), she made young women model themselves to death.† Prior to the San Francisco screening of *Mondo Trasho* (1969), Divine, billed as the most beautiful woman in the world, did a live nightclub act in which she threw fish, had "glamour fits" (exhibitionist poses coupled with temper tantrums), and strangled a policeman. (The audience cheered.) Waters's humor, the director insists, "is based on nervous reactions to anxiety-provoking situations" (94), including ones that provoke the male sexual anxiety to which Garafola alludes. But in *Female Trouble*, the cheers Dawn receives at the end of a similar act—

---

*Dawn is a fashion victim who weighs three hundred pounds and has been disfigured by horrendous make-up, acid thrown in her face, and hairdos only a Baltimorean would appreciate.

†Waters claims they collapse from "fashion exhaustion" (52).

Dawn flips on a trampoline, tears apart a telephone book, and rubs herself with fish—become screams when, in a Maria Montez moment, she declares herself to be "so fucking beautiful I can't stand it myself" and fires a pistol into the audience for the sake of art. It's a blood bath that causes a riot reminiscent of *Le Sacre du printemps* and a crime that lands Dawn in the electric chair.

New York, 1916

MUSIC: STRAUSS

LIBRETTO: NIJINSKY

CHOREOGRAPHY: NIJINSKY

SETS AND COSTUMES: JONES

❧

Tyl Eulenspiegel

Nijinsky gave Tyl the last laugh, resurrecting himself in the irrepressible role. Closing with Strauss, Nijinsky had Tyl killed in the prime of life. Opening Strauss up, he had Tyl, like Petrouchka, survive his death. To quote one review:

So far Strauss, the attributed program to his rondo, the evergreen traditions of the "merry pranks" that the composer has sent from Bavaria world-wide. Then, for climax, the wry, the comic, the modern rather than the medieval, the finely touched and the finely stimulating invention of Mr. Nijinsky himself. Nightfall comes: the respectable are at home and abed; only the rabble, fed, happy, elated, intoxicated with the happenings of Til's afternoon, haunt the square. Regardless of what Strauss's music may or may not imply, heedless of the tradition that the radical Nijinsky has thrown to the winds, they acclaim and enthrone him as their deliverer. On the shoulders of the mob sits Til, enthroned, the sovereign of the wit that brings freedom, of the mockery that sends conventions and hypocrisies toppling down. Respectable Braunschweig and disregarded Strauss may endure no more. Into the "public place" troop the Inquisitors; back to Til's trial and hanging comes the tone-poem. Then and there he is strung up—red light of warning. But no sooner are the executioners gone than he springs anew into being, the perpetual being of the humor that bursts sham, the jeer

that pricks pretension. Wistfully, prophetically—to
Strauss's epilogue—the rabble eyes a perennial miracle.
(H. T. Parker, "The Russians in Full Glory," *Boston
Evening Transcript*, Nov. 7, 1916)

Robert Edmond Jones, who did the decor, was transfixed as well, extolling the glee with which this "chameleon"—"Til the imp, Til the lover, Til the scholar, Til flouting, taunting, imploring, writhing in his death agonies"—summoned the spirits of Breughel, Munchhausen, and Rabelais and likening the final apparition, in which Tyl emerged from a group of grieving women in a flight of balloons, to "a moth veering above a sea of fireflies" (51, 60). Van Vechten concurred: "Nijinsky was quite justified in altering the end of the work, which hangs the rogue-hero, into another practical joke [because] the keynote of Nijinsky's interpretation was gaiety" ("Russian Ballet" 11).

Gaiety, not gayness. As Garafola remarks, once "Nijinsky's ambisexual youth . . . met his end" in the Chosen One's death, "the heroes of his ballets [had] conventional masculine identities" (*Diaghilev* 71–72). Tyl simply isn't one of the roles nor is his innovative resurrection one of the gestures with which (homosexual) gay men, let alone gay critics, concern themselves. But he should be. Nijinsky's final ludic performance is an exemplary instance of the cultural work queer theorists, myself included (up to now, at any rate), still hope—wistfully, if not prophetically—to accomplish. Like Barthes, another French performance artist whose final texts have been opened by Americans, Nijinsky's Tyl knows we're all chameleons—knows in other words that our stereotypical selves, including our sexual selves, are, like my narcissism, both performative and constrictive. Like Barthes, he shows us how to act upon—or act out—that knowledge, thereby liberating ourselves. And he proves, more convincingly than either Barthes or Petrouchka, how exhilarating that liberation can be.

St. Moritz, 1919

MUSIC: CHOPIN

CHOREOGRAPHY: NIJINSKY

*E*verything pales in the face of war. Everything but love, according to some—whatever love is. It's a notion Nijinsky touched on in his final, death-driven, guilt-ridden, and fully mad performance. "Now I will dance you the war, with its suffering, with its destruction, with its death," he told his audience. "The war which you did not prevent and so you are also responsible for." According to Romola, Nijinsky did "fill the room with horror-stricken suffering humanity."

> It was tragic; his gestures were all monumental, and he entranced us so that we almost saw him floating over corpses. The public sat breathlessly horrified and so strangely fascinated. They seemed to be petrified. But we felt that Vaslav was like one of those overpowering creatures full of dominating strength, a tiger let out from the jungle who in any moment could destroy us. And he was dancing, dancing on. Whirling through space, taking his audience away with him to war, to destruction, facing suffering and horror, struggling with all his steel-like muscles, his agility, his lightning quickness, his ethereal being, to escape the inevitable end. It was the dance for life against death. (425–26)

Or for love against death. To quote the diary entry Nijinsky wrote that evening: "They were afraid of me, thinking I wanted to kill them. I did not. I loved everybody but nobody loved me" (161).

It's an entry Bidart touches upon in "The War of Vaslav
Nijinsky."

Still gripped by the illusion of an horizon;
overcome with the finality of a broken tooth;
suspecting that habits are the only salvation,

—the Nineteenth Century's
guilt, *World War One*,

was danced

by Nijinsky on January 19, 1919.

•   •   •

. . . I am now reading *Ecce Homo*. Nietzsche
is *angry* with me—;

he hates "the Crucified One."

But he did not live through War—;
when the whole world painted its face

with blood.

Someone must expiate the blood.

•   •   •

No. Let what is past
be forgotten. Let even the blood

be forgotten—; there *can be no* "expiation."

Expiation is not necessary.

Suffering has made me what I am,—

I must not regret; or judge; or
struggle to escape it

in the indifference of (the ruthless
ecstasy of)

> CHANGE; "my endless RENEWAL";
> BECOMING.

—That is Nietzsche.

He wants to say *"Yes"* to life.

I am not Nietzsche. I am the bride of Christ.

•　　　•　　　•

He was planning a new and original ballet. It was to be
a picture of sex life, with the scene laid in a *maison
tolérée*. The chief character was to be the owner—once
a beautiful *cocotte*, now aged and paralyzed as a result
of her debauchery; but, though her body is a wreck, her
spirit is indomitable in the traffic of love. She deals with
all the wares of love, selling girls to boys, youth to age,
woman to woman, man to man.

When he danced it, he succeeded in transmitting the
whole scale of sex life.

•　　　•　　　•

—Many times Diaghilev wanted me
to make love to him

as if he were
a woman—;

I did. I *refuse* to
regret it.

      At first, I felt humiliated for him,—

he saw this. He got angry
and said, "I enjoy it!"

Then, more calmly, he said,

"Vatza, we must not *regret* what we *feel*."

—I REGRETTED

        what I FELT . . . Not

making love, but that since the beginning
I wanted to *leave* him . . .

        That I stayed

out of "GRATITUDE,"—

        and *FEAR OF LIFE*,—

          and AMBITION . . .

That in my soul,

        I did *not* love him. (21–23)

Auden, the day World War II was declared, opened Nijin-sky's diary and found a related passage: "Some politicians are hypocrites like Diaghilev, who does not want universal love, but to be loved alone. I want universal love" [27]. It's an entry Auden touched upon in "September 1, 1939."

The windiest militant trash
Important Persons shout
Is not so crude as our wish:
What mad Nijinsky wrote
About Diaghilev
Is true of the normal heart;
For the error bred in the bone
Of each woman and each man
Craves what it cannot have,
Not universal love
But to be loved alone . . . .

All I have is a voice
To undo the folded lie,
The romantic lie in the brain
Of the sensual man-in-the-street
And the lie of Authority
Whose buildings grope the sky:
There is no such thing as the State
And no one exists alone;
Hunger allows no choice
To the citizen or the police;
We must love one another or die. (88)

The final line is famous. Forster, for one, felt that because Auden "once wrote 'We must love one another or die,' he can command me to follow him" (quoted in Mendelson 326). Auden himself, however, came to view the line as dishonest, both because we die whether or not we love one another and because the kind of love he values isn't a "hunger," an instinctive—or purely sensual—need. Rather, it's a gift we bestow as a form of forgiveness. In other words, *Christian* love, for Auden as for Nijinsky ("the bride of Christ")—but for the rest of us, not necessarily so. For Larry Kramer, for example, the love that can save us from the horror of a war we're still fighting—the war against both AIDS and homophobia—is *Judeo*-Christian. To quote Kramer's alter ego in *The Normal Heart* (a play the title and epigraph of which are taken from "September 1, 1939" and the essence of which producer Joseph Papp called "love holding firm under fire, put to the ultimate test, facing and overcoming . . . death" [29]), the struggle to remind people that gay culture "isn't just sexual" (114) and to be remembered by them as one who fought the war is "part of what it means to be Jewish" (113). Not that it matters. For if love, in fact, ever does the trick, all such distinctions—between love and lust, normal and abnormal, Christian and Jew, heterosexual and homosexual—will have been pointless for quite some time.

Reinscription

I sign this book with Nijinsky's name, not my own. You see and hear very little in Kevin Kopelson. Only the symmetry of K——n / K——n, and the explosiveness of consonants that don't agree with me. But Vaslav Nijinsky is a name the homographesis of which we've known for years. Genet, for example, sensed Nijinsky's lightness in the word: "the rise of the N, the drop of the loop of the j, the leap of the hook on the k and the fall of the y, graphic form of a name that seems to be drawing the artist's élan, with its bounds and rebounds on the boards, of the jumper who doesn't know which leg to come down on" (173). Rorem, not surprisingly, senses an Eliotic autobiographesis:

> Did I mention that Laurence Olivier and Vivien Leigh, already a mythological pair in early 1940, performed *Romeo and Juliet* in the drafty Auditorium Theater, after the Ballets Russes had left, but no one could hear a word. (Twenty-five years later, when Olivier had his face-lift, he told John Houseman who told Virgil [Thomson] who told me: "I looked so good I wanted to go down on myself.") Did I mention that Ella Fitzgerald's way with words was a way culled from the twenties and stretching outmodedly into the sixties: she put a mordant—a sort of tilde à la Falla—on unimportant words like "the" as well as on important words like "love"? Or like Debussy's self-conscious setting of the word "nu," with a little trill, in *Placet futile*. Or like Genet's comparing Nijinsky's dancing to his name:

the dotted j twixt the two dotted i's sinks and rises in jerky slow motion. (Mae Swenson once in a poem drew our attention to the same iji, hoping, I suppose, that we wouldn't have seen it already chez Genet.)

Can there be a shape to a memoir other than through the straight line toward death by natural causes (which includes accident, suicide, and murder)? We always die alone, yes, but we live alone too. Since Man has no soul (though certain animals have), shape is moot, does not exist in nature, and the memoir will sink and rise in jerky slow motion, arbitrarily, like some negligible detail out of the Big Bang or, more likely, the Big Whimper. (136–37)

Koestenbaum, however, who deserves the final word, senses other qualities as well: "I've always heard the 'jinx' and 'djinn' in 'Nijinsky,'" he once told me, "always loved the 'iji,' the three dotted letters 'i' and 'j' and 'i' all in a row, the 'sky' in Nijinsky, too, and I believe the name is magical."

Reference Matter

Acocella, Joan. "Heroes and Hero Worship." Review of Lincoln Kirstein, *Mosaic: Memoirs*. *New York Review of Books* 42, 18 (Nov. 16, 1995): 30–35.

Acton, Harold. *Memoirs of an Aesthete*. London: Methuen, 1948.

Albright, Ann Cooper. "Incalculable Choreographies: The Dance Practice of Marie Chouinard." In *Bodies of the Text: Dance as Theory, Literature as Dance*, ed. Ellen W. Goellner and Jacqueline Shea Murphy, 157–81. New Brunswick, N.J.: Rutgers University Press, 1995.

Auden, W. H. "September 1, 1939." In *Selected Poems: New Edition*, 86–89. Ed. Edward Mendelson. New York: Vintage, 1979.

Barbier, George. *Nijinsky*. Trans. Cyril W. Beaumont. London: Beaumont, 1913.

Barthes, Roland. *Mythologies*. Trans. Annette Lavers. New York: Hill & Wang, 1972. Orig. pub. in French 1957.

———. *Roland Barthes by Roland Barthes*. Trans. Richard Howard. New York: Hill & Wang, 1977. Orig. pub. in French 1975.

Beaumont, Cyril W. *The Diaghilev Ballet in London*. London: Putnam, 1940.

Benois, Alexandre. *Reminiscences of the Russian Ballet*. Trans. Mary Britnieva. London: Putnam, 1941.

Bersani, Leo. "Is the Rectum a Grave?" In *AIDS: Cultural Analysis, Cultural Activism*, ed. Douglas Crimp, 197–222. Cambridge, Mass.: MIT, 1988.

Bidart, Frank. "The War of Vaslav Nijinsky" [1983]. In *In the*

Western Night: Collected Poems 1965–90, 21–49. New York: Farrar, Straus & Giroux, 1990.

Bourman, Anatole. *The Tragedy of Nijinsky*. New York: Mc-Graw-Hill, 1936.

Buckle, Richard. *Nijinsky*. New York: Simon & Schuster, 1971.

Burt, Ramsay. *The Male Dancer: Bodies, Spectacle, Sexualities*. London: Routledge, 1995.

Cocteau, Jean. *Dessins*. Paris: Stock, 1924.

———. *The Journals of Jean Cocteau*. Trans. Wallace Fowlie. New York: Criterion, 1956.

———. *Past Tense*. Vol. 2 of *Diaries*. Trans. Richard Howard. New York: Harcourt Brace Jovanovich, 1987.

Cocteau, Jean, and Alexandre Arséne. *The Decorative Art of Léon Bakst*. Trans. Harry Melvill. New York: Benjamin Blom, 1971. Orig. pub. in French 1913.

Cohen, Marshall. "Primitivism, Modernism, and Dance Theory" [1981]. In *What Is Dance?*, ed. Roger Copeland and Marshall Cohen, 161–78. Oxford: Oxford University Press, 1983.

Denby, Edwin. "Carmen Amaya; Isadora Reconsidered; Dance Photographs; 'Punch and the Judy' Revisited" [1942]. In *Dance Writings*, 86–92. Ed. Robert Cornfield and William MacKay. New York: Knopf, 1986.

———. "Flight of the Dancer" [1943]. In *Dance Writings*, 501–5. Ed. Robert Cornfield and William MacKay. New York: Knopf, 1986.

———. "Nijinsky's 'Faun'; Massine's 'Symphonie Fantastique'; American Ballet Caravan" [1936]. In *Dance Writings*, 38–41. Ed. Robert Cornfield and William MacKay. New York: Knopf, 1986.

———. "Notes on Nijinsky Photographs" [1946]. In *Nijinsky, Pavlova, Duncan: Three Lives in Dance*, ed. Paul Magriel, 15–21. New York: Da Capo, 1977.

————. "'Schéhérazade': A Foundering Warhorse" [1944]. In *Dance Writings*, 239–40. Ed. Robert Cornfield and William MacKay. New York: Knopf, 1986.

Edelman, Lee. *Homographesis: Essays in Gay Literary and Cultural Theory*. New York: Routledge, 1994.

English, Rose. "Alas, Alack." *New Dance* 15 (1980): 18–19.

Eyman, Scott. *Mary Pickford: America's Sweetheart*. New York: Donald I. Fine, 1990.

Firbank, Ronald. *The Flower Beneath the Foot*. In *Five Novels*. New York: New Directions, 1961. Orig pub. 1923.

Fokine, Michel. *Memoirs of a Ballet Master*. Trans. Vitale Fokine. Ed. Anatole Chujoy. Boston: Little, Brown, 1961.

Ford, Charles Henri, and Parker Tyler. *The Young and Evil*. New York: Gay Presses of New York, 1988. Orig. pub. 1933.

Galipaux, Félix. "Comment on monte une pantomine." In Félix Larcher and Paul Hugounet, *Les Soirées funambulesques: Notes et documents inédits pour servir à l'histoire de la pantomime*. Paris: Kolb, 1890–93.

Garafola, Lynn. *Diaghilev's Ballets Russes*. Oxford: Oxford University Press, 1989.

————. "Vaslav Nijinsky." *Raritan* 8, 1 (Summer 1988): 1–27.

The Gay Pillow Book. San Francisco: HarperCollins, 1995.

Genet, Jean. *Our Lady of the Flowers*. Trans. Bernard Frechtman. New York: Grove, 1963. Orig. pub. in French 1943.

Gifford, Barry. *Landscape with Traveler: The Pillow Book of Francis Reeves*. New York: Vintage, 1993. Orig. pub. 1980.

Girard, René. "Scandal and the Dance: Salome in the Gospel of Mark." *New Literary History* 15, 2 (Winter 1984): 311–24.

Hahn, Reynaldo. *Le Dieu bleu*, piano score. Paris: Hengel, 1911.

Hay, Harry. "Origins of Modern Dance." Letter to the Editor. *Harvard Gay and Lesbian Review* 2, 3 (Summer 1995): 52.

Hocquenghem, Guy. *L'Après-Mai des faunes*. Paris: Grasset, 1974.

Hofmannsthal, Hugo von. "Nijinskys 'Nachmittag eines Fauns'" [1912]. *Prosa*. 4 vols. 3: 145–48. Frankfurt: S. Fischer, 1950–55.

Holroyd, Michael. *Lytton Strachey: A Critical Biography*. 2 vols. New York: Holt, Rhinehart & Winston, 1968.

Jacobs, Peter. "'Quel décor!' Nijinsky Conquers Bloomsbury." *Charleston Magazine* 9 (Spring/Summer 1994): 15–19.

Johnson, A. E. *The Russian Ballet*. London: Constable, 1913.

Jones, Robert Edmond. "Nijinsky and Til Eulenspiegel." In *Nijinsky, Pavlova, Duncan: Three Lives in Dance*, ed. Paul Magriel, 46–60. New York: Da Capo, 1977.

Karsavina, Tamara. *Theatre Street*. New York: Dutton, 1961. Orig. pub. 1930.

Kirstein, Lincoln. "Classical Ballet: Aria of the Aerial" [1976]. In *What Is Dance?*, ed. Roger Copeland and Marshall Cohen, 238–43. Oxford: Oxford University Press, 1983.

———. *Mosaic: Memoirs*. New York: Farrar, Straus & Giroux, 1994.

———. *Nijinsky Dancing*. London: Thames and Hudson, 1975.

Koestenbaum, Wayne. "Fugitive Blue," In *Ode to Anna Moffo and Other Poems*, 9–11. New York: Persea, 1990.

———. "Shéhérazade." In *Ode to Anna Moffo and Other Poems*, 3–8. New York: Persea, 1990.

Kopelson, Kevin. *Love's Litany: The Writing of Modern Homoerotics*. Stanford, Calif.: Stanford University Press, 1994.

Kramer, Larry. *The Normal Heart*. New York: Plume, 1985.

Krasovskaya, Vera. *Nijinsky*. Trans. John E. Bowlt. New York: Schirmer-Macmillan, 1979.

Levinson, André. *Bakst: The Story of the Artist's Life*. London, 1923.

———. "O moskovskom balete." *Apollon* 10 (1911): 160.

Lieven, Prince Peter. *Birth of Ballets Russes*. Trans. L. Zarine. Boston: Houghton Mifflin, 1936.

Mann, Thomas. *Death in Venice*. Trans. H. T. Lowe-Porter. London: Penguin, 1971. Orig. pub. in German 1912.

Massine, Léonide. *My Life in Ballet*. Ed. Phyllis Hartnoll and Robert Rubens. London: Macmillan, 1968.

McClary, Susan. "Music, the Pythagoreans, and the Body." In *Choreographing History*, ed. Susan Leigh Foster, 82–104. Bloomington: Indiana University Press, 1995.

Mendelson, Edward. *Early Auden*. Cambridge, Mass.: Harvard University Press, 1983.

Mendès, Catulle. *L'Art au théâtre, deuxieme année* (1896). Paris: Charpentier-Fasquelle, 1897.

Miomandre, Francis de. Introduction to *Dessins sur les danses de Vaslav Nijinsky*, by George Barbier. Paris: Bernouard, 1912.

Misler, Nicoletta. "Siamese Dancing and the Ballets Russes." In *The Art of Enchantment: Diaghilev's Ballets Russes 1909–1929*, ed. Nancy Van Norman Baer, 78–83. New York: Universe, 1988.

Moon, Michael. "Flaming Closets." In *Bodies of the Text: Dance as Theory, Literature as Dance*, ed. Ellen W. Goellner and Jacqueline Shea Murphy, 57–78. New Brunswick, N.J.: Rutgers University Press, 1995.

Morrell, Ottoline. *Memoirs of Lady Ottoline Morrell: A Study in Friendship, 1873–1915*. Ed. Robert Gathorne-Hardy. New York: Knopf, 1964.

Néagu, Philippe, Jean-Michel Nectoux, Claudia Jeschke, and Ann Hutchinson Guest. *Afternoon of a Faun: Mallarmé, Debussy, Nijinsky*. Ed. Jean-Michel Nectoux. Trans. Maximilian Vos. New York, Paris: Vendome, 1987.

Nietzsche, Friedrich. *'The Birth of Tragedy' and 'The Genealogy of Morals'*. Trans. Francis Golffing. Garden City: Doubleday, 1956.

Nijinska, Bronislava. *Early Memoirs*. Trans. Irina Nijinska and Jean Rawlinson. London: Faber & Faber, 1981.

Nijinsky, Romola. *Nijinsky*. New York: Simon & Schuster, 1968. Orig. pub. 1934.

Nijinsky, Vaslav. *The Diary of Vaslav Nijinsky*. Ed. Romola Nijinsky. Berkeley: University of California Press, 1968. Orig. pub. 1936.

Painter, George D. *Marcel Proust: A Biography*. 2 vols. New York: Random House / Vintage, 1978.

Papp, Joseph. Foreword to *The Normal Heart*, by Larry Kramer. New York: Plume, 1985.

Pater, Walter. *The Renaissance: Studies in Art and Poetry*. New York: Macmillan, 1907. Orig. pub. 1873.

Phelps, Robert. *Professional Secrets*. Trans. Richard Howard. New York: Farrar, Straus & Giroux, 1970.

Pound, Ezra. "Les Millwin" [1913]. In *Personae: The Shorter Poems*, 94. New York: New Directions, 1990.

Preminger, Otto. *Preminger: An Autobiography*. Garden City: Doubleday, 1977.

Proust, Marcel. *The Captive*. In vol. 3 of *Remembrance of Things Past*. Trans. C. K. Scott Moncrieff and Terence Kilmartin. New York: Random House / Vintage, 1982.

———. *Cities of the Plain*. In vol. 2 of *Remembrance of Things Past*. Trans. C. K. Scott Moncrieff and Terence Kilmartin. New York: Random House / Vintage, 1982.

———. *Time Regained*. In vol. 3. of *Remembrance of Things Past*. Trans. C. K. Scott Moncrieff and Terence Kilmartin. New York: Random House / Vintage, 1982.

Ravel, Maurice. "Nijinsky as Ballet Master." In *A Ravel Reader: Correspondence, Articles, Interviews*, ed. Arbie Orenstein, 404–5. New York: Columbia University Press, 1990.

Reiss, Françoise. *Nijinsky: A Biography*. London: A. & C. Black, 1960.

Ricketts, Charles. *Self-Portrait: Taken from the Letters and Journals.* Ed. Cecil Lewis and Sturge Moore. London: Peter Davies, 1939.

Ries, Frank W. D. *The Dance Theatre of Jean Cocteau.* Ann Arbor: UMI Research, 1986.

Rorem, Ned. *Knowing When to Stop: A Memoir.* New York: Simon & Schuster, 1994.

Rosen, Charles. *The Romantic Generation.* Cambridge, Mass.: Harvard University Press, 1995.

Rozanov, Vasily. "Balet ruk" and "Zanimatel'nyi vecher." *Mir iskusstva* 1 (1901): 43–48.

Scholl, Tim. *From Petipa to Balanchine: Classical Revival and the Modernization of Ballet.* London: Routledge, 1994.

Sévérin. *L'Homme blanc: Souvenirs d'un Pierrot.* Ed. Gustave Fréjaville. Paris: Plon, 1929.

Siegel, Marcia. *Watching the Dance Go By.* Boston: Houghton Mifflin, 1977.

Sontag, Susan. "Notes on Camp" [1964]. In *Against Interpretation and Other Essays,* 275–92. New York: Farrar, Straus & Giroux, 1982.

Storey, Robert. *Pierrots on the Stage of Desire: Nineteenth-Century French Literary Artists and the Comic Pantomime.* Princeton, N.J.: Princeton University Press, 1985.

Stuart, Otis. *Perpetual Motion: The Public and Private Lives of Rudolf Nureyev.* New York: Simon & Schuster, 1995.

Studlar, Gaylyn. "Douglas Fairbanks: Thief of the Ballets Russes." In *Bodies of the Text: Dance as Theory, Literature as Dance,* ed. Ellen W. Goellner and Jacqueline Shea Murphy, 107–24. New Brunswick, N.J.: Rutgers University Press, 1995.

Turnbaugh, Douglas Blair. *Duncan Grant and the Bloomsbury Group.* Secaucus, N.J.: Lyle Stuart, 1987.

———. *Private: The Erotic Art of Duncan Grant 1885–1978.* London: Gay Men's, 1989.

Tytell, John. *Ezra Pound: The Solitary Volcano.* New York: Doubleday, 1987.

Van Vechten, Carl. *The Blind Bow-Boy.* New York: Knopf, 1923.

———. *Peter Whiffle: His Life and Works.* London: Grant Richards, 1923.

———. "The Russian Ballet and Nijinsky" [1916]. In *Nijinsky, Pavlova, Duncan: Three Lives in Dance*, ed. Paul Magriel, 1–14. New York: Da Capo, 1977.

———. "Secret of the Russian Ballet" [1915]. In *The Dance Writings of Carl Van Vechten*, 59–79. Ed. Paul Padgette. New York: Dance Horizons, 1974.

Verlaine, Paul. *Oeuvres en prose complètes.* Ed. Jacques Borel. Paris: Gallimard (Pléiade), 1972.

———. *Oeuvres poétiques complètes.* Ed. Y.-G. Le Dantec. Gallimard (Pléiade), 1977.

Waters, John. *Shock Value.* New York: Thunder's Mouth, 1981.

Watkins, Glenn. *Pyramids at the Louvre: Music, Culture, and Collage from Stravinsky to the Postmodernists.* Cambridge, Mass.: Harvard University Press, 1994.

Whitworth, Geoffrey. *The Art of Nijinsky.* London: Chatto & Windus, 1913.

Wilde, Oscar. "The Ballad of Reading Gaol" [1898]. In *The Complete Illustrated Stories, Plays and Poems of Oscar Wilde*, 843–60. London: Chancellor, 1986.

———. "Phrases and Philosophies for the Use of the Young" [1894]. In *The Complete Illustrated Stories, Plays and Poems of Oscar Wilde*, 1205–6. London: Chancellor, 1986.

Wollen, Peter. "Fashion / Orientalism / The Body." *New Formations* 1 (Spring 1987): 5–33.

Library of Congress Cataloging-in-Publication Data

Kopelson, Kevin

The queer afterlife of Vaslav Nijinsky / Kevin Kopelson

    p.   cm.

Includes bibliographical references.

ISBN 0-8047-2949-2 (cloth)—ISBN 0-8047-2950-6 (pbk.)

   1. Nijinsky, Waslaw, 1890–1950. 2. Homosexuality. 3. Gesture in
dance—Psychological aspects. I. Title.

GV1785.N6K66   1997

792.8'2'092—dc21

[B]   97-13449

                                              CIP

Original printing 1997

Last figure below indicates year of this printing:

06   05   04   03   02   01   00   99   98   97